PRAISE FOR
BEFORE THE MIC

"This book wisely addresses 'style over substance'—the former, vacuous without first attending to the raw material. Once that's in place, everything else will flow ... and deliver. The use of songwriting as an analogy—i.e. the creation of original material, straight from the heart—is a recurring theme throughout this brilliant book of ideas and life-changing advice on how to write captivating presentations."

—RORY MACDONALD, songwriter from
Celtic rock band Runrig

"Glenn Gibson provides the reader with a concise, well-organized guide to preparing oneself to deliver a high-impact presentation to any audience. Full of helpful tips and preparation tools, this is required reading for both experienced and inexperienced speakers."

—WILLIAM D. SULLIVAN, Vice Admiral, US Navy (Retired)

"Of the thousands of presentations I have seen over the course of my thirty-year career, Glenn Gibson has delivered or helped write some of the very best. Glenn's coaching and collaboration have been invaluable to my development as an effective presenter, which is an essential competency of any organizational leader."

—BILL PRIEMER, president and CEO, Hyland

"I have been awed by many of Glenn's presentations over the years, and I'm thrilled he is sharing his method in *Before the Mic*. Whether you love getting in front of audiences or the thought makes your stomach flip (like it does mine!), this book will give you a step-by-step process to build and deliver a message that resonates and remains with your audience. If you want what you present to matter, *Before the Mic* is the book for you. Glenn's advice goes beyond presentation skills and offers actionable steps to help you figure out what you want to say and then how to say it so it matters to the audience."

–MARY MCKNIGHT, CEO, Next Phase Solutions, LLC

"I've given hundreds of keynotes in my career. No matter how many presentations you've given—and no matter how good you think you are—you'll find great advice and motivation in *Before the Mic*. Read it now, before you make your next presentation, whether it's for small group of colleagues or an audience of thousands."

–JOHN MANCINI, president of Content Results, LLC

"I have had the privilege of hearing Glenn speak more than a dozen times over the past decade. Each and every time, Glenn has found a way to teach in a memorable and entertaining way, and now I know his secrets! Glenn's book is as polished, professional, and engaging as his presentations."

–MICHAEL CARR, president and CEO, Naviant, Inc.

"This book is the secret sauce to being an aMMMazing presenter. The guidance presented by Gibson is spot-on. It captures all the elements of how to create an aMMMazing presentation in an easy-to-consume and actionable workbook format. A must-have for anyone who has to get up in front of an audience and tell a story!"

−MARISA KOPEC, CEO and founder,
Winning Methodologies, LLC

"The ability to effectively communicate in a group setting is a fundamental skill to a successful career. Glenn expertly unlocks the keys that you will learn to propel your career to the next level."

−JIM WANNER, chief expectations officer, KeyMark, Inc.

"Glenn is an amazingly captivating presenter who has mastered the art of building a presentation. *Before the Mic* is a must-read for any salesperson looking to grab and keep their prospect's attention . . . and compel them to take action! In a world where deals are won or lost over videoconferencing, this critical skillset has become more important than ever. Glenn teaches his readers the new way to create a rockstar presentation every time!"

−JENIFER HEIN, marketing director, Naviant, Inc.

"He [Glenn Gibson] is one of the most gifted presenters I've ever encountered, and I am fortunate enough to have him as a colleague. Let's be honest. Most presenters aren't very good. Those that are good usually do a nice job of keeping you engaged. But it is a precious few presenters that are truly memorable. People think that memorable presentations equate to big personalities, or great use of graphics or videos. Truly memorable presentations, though, come from meticulous preparation, understanding your audience, the subject matter, and the goals you have for the audience to take away from the presentation. That is what Glenn does better than anyone I've seen. So, before your next presentation, learn how Glenn used these methods to turn an introduction of a juggling act (seriously) to a crowd of 2,500 people into one of the best customer presentations I've ever seen."

–ED MCQUISTON, chief operating officer, Hyland

"We learned so much from this amazingly helpful book. Glenn Gibson's book focuses on the most important part of a speech: the writing. This book is clear, instructive, and teaches his excellent approach to writing the presentation you really want to give. Everyone who writes speeches can learn something from this book. Read it, do what Glenn says, and you will write excellent, effective, emotional presentations."

–JON WEE AND **OWEN MORSE,** comedy and
juggling duo, The Passing Zone

"The perfect book to recommend to anyone and everyone who is involved in delivering successful and effective presentations. It's an essential gem that you not only read but can actually use! Easy to read, nicely illustrated, packed full of practical, no-nonsense, tried-and-tested advice, guidance, helpful templates, and easy-to-use tools. Brilliant!"

-STUART RICHARDSON, businessman, entrepreneur, and author of the TRIM course

"The concepts shared in *Before the Mic* have fundamentally changed the way I present. I am able to more confidently present to small group meetings all the way up to audiences of thousands. Read this book! It will help you to write Meaningful, Memorable, and Motivational presentations!"

-JOHN PHELAN, chief product officer, Hyland

"When he is in front of the mic, Glenn's superpower is his ability to draw in and delight the audience. Though we can't learn his charm, in Glenn's new book we can learn his techniques on how to make every presentation meaningful and memorable."

-RACHEL YOUNG, marketing executive, former Forrester SiriusDecisions portfolio marketing research

"Glenn has always been my 'go-to' person when I'm creating key presentations. He provides that perfect insight to ensure your message hits its audience with a bullseye. Watching Glenn deliver a presentation is always amazing. Make no mistake; it is not just the allure of the Scottish accent that makes Glenn a killer presenter. He understands how to deliver a compelling message with actionable takeaways for the audience."

-SAM BABIC, chief innovation officer, Hyland

"Glenn Gibson is a natural, talented presentation artist who has developed a scientific formula to creating aMMMazing presentations. His tried-and-true approach is quick to model and easy to learn. Glenn's methods are honed by years of experience, research, and practice, which has turned his artistic gift into a repeatable science that we can all follow to create aMMMazing presentations each and every time!"

—AMY MAXEY, manager, global conferences and events, Hyland

"I have had the pleasure to see Glenn speak live on many occasions. I cannot think of another person who does a better job captivating an audience and making each and every presentation fun and exciting! It is great to see his talents captured as a resource for us all to improve such an important skill!"

—MATT CHARLSON, CEO, Databank

"This book will improve your performance in front of people. Glenn's unique insight into how to perfect your presentations coupled with his musical analogies make this is a must-read!"

—MARK GRIMES, comedian and actor

"Transforming the experience of public speaking from drudgery to privilege, that is the magic of Glenn Gibson. In this beautifully written book you're sure to quickly learn the unique, meaningful, and lasting approach to coaching anyone to honor the microphone. Keep it simple, make it relatable, and have fun. Dig in!"

—BRENDA KIRK, CIO

BEFORE THE MIC

HOW TO COMPOSE MEANINGFUL, MEMORABLE, AND MOTIVATIONAL PRESENTATIONS

Written and Illustrated by

GLENN GIBSON

RIVER GROVE
BOOKS

Published by River Grove Books
Austin, TX
www.rivergrovebooks.com

Distributed by River Grove Books

Design and composition by Greenleaf Book Group
Cover design by Greenleaf Book Group
Cover images: The microphone for the stage stands on a stand on a black
background; microphone on a dark background with smoke used under
license from Shutterstock.com

Publisher's Cataloging-in-Publication data is available.

Print ISBN: 978-1-63299-364-9

eBook ISBN: 978-1-63299-365-6

First Edition

To my dad, Alistair, who always encouraged me to be fearless before the microphone, and to my boys, Finlay and Oran, who I hope to inspire to do the same.

CONTENTS

APPENDIX: TOOLS AND TEMPLATES

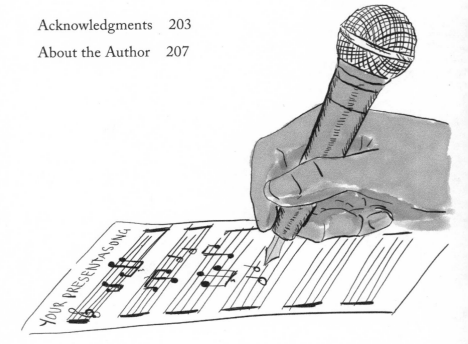

PREFACE

HELLO THERE! THERE ARE HUNDREDS of books available on the topic of presentations, so why should you read this one?

After decades of examining the art and science of presentations through reading, doing, and observing, I realized that many books touch on topics across the entire spectrum of presentations—what to say, how to say it, what your slides should look like, how to appear confident, how to handle questions, and how to generally be a superstar in front of a live audience. It would be overwhelming to try to improve in all of these areas at the same time, but on top of that, I noticed a lack of advice around the hardest and most time-intensive part of the whole experience—the actual *writing* process.

I've built a career out of writing presentations, for myself and for others. Over the past twenty years, I've composed thousands of presentations, which have been delivered to audiences numbering into the thousands at a range of in-person and virtual industry conferences, events, and training sessions around the world.

Over the years, I've honed a repeatable methodology that I use to write all of my presentations, and I've created a range of tools, templates, and tricks to help me create my words and visuals quickly while working on multiple projects and presentations simultaneously. I have trained hundreds of executives and sales professionals using this methodology, and I've used it to write keynotes, sales pitches, board presentations, and even eulogies, commencements, and wedding speeches!

I've also been privileged to pick up several presentation awards[1] along the way.

I decided to write down my methodology and include it in a book that is different from those others by focusing on just one aspect of presentations, arguably the most important aspect to get right *first*: the writing process. This book concentrates on all of the work and preparation necessary to get you ready before the mic is in your hand.

I set out to write this book in the same way that I would approach writing a presentation on the very same topic. As I jammed out my ideas, I used the very tools, methodologies, and best practices that are contained within these pages, what I call the aMMMazing presentation theory. I also held myself accountable to apply the principles of aMMMazing presentations throughout each section.

In this book, I've culled all of my years of professional knowledge to help anyone create stronger presentations, every time. This book takes an approach that can best be described as "words first, visuals last." This method will help you focus on writing captivating presentations, which can then be delivered with or without the aid of a slide deck in any delivery setting. When you do need

---

1   List of Presentation Awards: Winner of Top Presenter Award, Hyland Software TechQuest Event, 2010 and 2011; Best Pitch, Tech Week North East Ohio Spin Association (NEOSA), 2012 and 2013; Most Wanted Product, Tech Week NEOSA, 2012 and 2013; Dale Carnegie Best Innovation Presentation 2018; Association of Intelligent Information Management Pitch Perfect Winner, 2016. Here's a link to my pitch: https://sharebase.onbase.com/en-AU/resources/press-releases/sharebase-by-hyland-wins-first-aiim-pitch-perfect-award.

accompanying visuals, this method will forever help you improve your slide decks, because you will create your slides to complement the words you've already written, not the other way around.

This has never been more important than it is now, in a world where presenting over video conferencing is the norm. In these situations, not only are you in a different *room* from your audience, you are now being given less time than ever to present.

In these situations, how do you grab and retain the attention of your audience, make your key points, and spur them to action in such a short window of time?

Not only will this book help you get your point across with beautiful words and simple visuals, but it will also help you figure out what your *point* is in the first place.

Whether you love speaking in front of others or you only do it because you have to, I wrote this book to help you increase your confidence in your material, which is the foundation of all other presentation skills.

Are you ready to learn how to compose captivating, aMMMazing presentations? Read on!

Glenn

INTRODUCTION

HOW DO YOU FEEL WHEN you are standing before the mic and about to begin speaking in front of a room full of people? Which of the following best describes you?

- ❏ Nervous
- ❏ Excited
- ❏ Terrified
- ❏ Energized
- ❏ Sweaty
- ❏ All of the above

Perhaps you don't present very often and the idea of public speaking fills you with dread. Or, on the other end of the spectrum, maybe you present all the time and you feel totally comfortable commanding the attention of a room or a video-conferencing session.

What if you learned that how you *feel* about speaking in front of an audience is irrelevant as to whether you can be effective at it or not? To understand what I mean, let me ask you a question.

How do you feel about singing karaoke?

When you see those neon lights advertising "Live Karaoke Tonight," are you like a moth to a flame, or would you march in the opposite direction? If you stumble into a bar with live karaoke, do you go seeking a tiny pencil to write down "Sweet Caroline," or do you lock yourself in the bathroom?

You might wonder, what does it matter? What on earth does karaoke have to do with presenting?

The obvious route is to draw a comparison between the karaoke singer reading the words from a monitor and the presenter who doesn't know what they are saying until the words appear on the projector screen. I could take this further and talk about how most slide decks (and Prezi canvases) should have a bouncing ball over the words for the presenter to follow, and then discuss how terrible that style of delivery is. But that is not the point of this book, even if it is true.

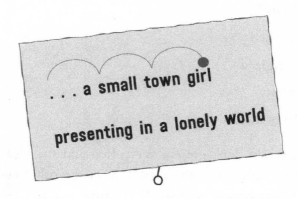

Whether you love or loathe karaoke, there is a direct comparison between singing and presenting.

Think about it.

In both situations, in person or in a video-conferencing session, you are going to—

1. "Take the stage" in front of a room full of people (some of whom you know and some you don't)

2. Take command of a microphone (literally or metaphorically)

3. Make sounds with your vocal cords

And in both situations when you begin, whether you like it or not, your audience will be—

4. Looking at you, observing your facial expressions and your physical movements

5. Listening to you, hearing the noises that are coming out of your mouth

6. Reacting to you, forming an opinion based on what they see and hear

For some, these facts are the very reasons they feel anxious when presenting (and perhaps also would never sing karaoke even if their lives depended on it). Those who enjoy performing in front of people find these same facts energizing.

Whether you are in front of a virtual audience or standing in front of a room full of people, let's consider a vital question:

Why doesn't it matter how we feel when all eyes in the audience are on us?

Imagine for a second that you are out for a night with your friends and you witness the most *amazing* karaoke singer you have ever seen. This person gets up with all the bravado and swagger of Mick Jagger, whips the crowd into a frenzy, and belts out songs with breathtaking soulfulness. All you can think is *What a performer!* You might reflect on your own stage presence and think, *I wish I was that confident in front of an audience.* You might even think about occasions when you get up in front of others to present and begin to reason, *If I want to be a really inspiring presenter, I need to have the swagger of Jagger! I need to focus my energy on my stage presence.*

My answer to that line of reasoning is NO! That's not true! That's not true at all!

Why? Because here's the unavoidable truth—and the critical point of this book: Even the most amazing karaoke singer in the world is not the person who actually wrote the song.

When you present, you are not just the performer—you are also the *composer.*

Composing a great song is a lot, lot harder than simply performing it. Anyone can get up and sing karaoke. But most karaoke lovers have never written even one song, never mind a great song or a timeless classic.

Similarly, anyone can get up in front of a room, click through a slide deck, and verbalize words as they appear on a screen, like a karaoke singer. But not everyone knows how to compose a presentation that is truly worth listening to.

THIS   BEFORE THIS

I have seen many confident presenters stroll on stage, work the room, add humor at all the right places, click through a lovely looking slide deck, and overall, be quite entertaining. Yet, when they are done, they have left me wondering what the point of it all was.

I've also seen presenters who, on their first impression, seem as though they will have a boring delivery style but have ended up delivering some of the most memorable, thought-provoking, motivational presentations I've ever heard.

Now, before any presentation aficionados start weeping and gnashing their teeth, I'm *not* claiming that the delivery style of the presenter is unimportant. I am saying that it is secondary to the composition of the presentation itself. The most incredible presenters out there have both: well-composed presentations delivered in entirely engaging ways. But there are plenty of brilliant presenters who, even though they are not the most attention-loving, spotlight-grabbing, or microphone-hogging kind of people, can still tell a great story and captivate the audience.

But what about slide design? Many presenters feel that if their slides could just look better, everything would be OK.

I've had many requests from people seeking help to turn their bullet-point-ridden slide decks into gorgeous graphics. They feel that if someone can help them do that, they'll have turned a boring presentation into an incredible one.

In engagements like that, I've noticed a consistent trend over the years: By asking some basic questions to understand what the presentation is trying to accomplish, we usually end up putting the existing deck to the side and instead focus our attention on the *content* and *structure* of the information. We rarely end up working (initially at least) on the design, look, or layout of the slides.

The point is that learning to compose a great presentation requires skills that have nothing to do with stage presence, graphic design, or even confidence in front of an audience. There is simply no point in working on (or even worrying about) your presentation style or the design of your PowerPoint deck, Keynote slides, or Prezi canvases until you learn how to write something great.

This book focuses on the concept of "substance before style."

STYLE   SUBSTANCE

To take a significant leap forward as a presenter, the first question that you need to ask yourself is not "How can I improve my PowerPoint game?" or "How can I increase my confidence in front of an audience?" The first question you need to figure out is "**Are the presentations I write worth *listening* to?**"

Are you already a confident presenter?

If so, cherish that natural ability but don't rely on it. It's easy to fall into the trap of "winging" presentations, throwing together some thoughts at the last minute, or relying on experience, confidence, and humor to get you through as you "speak to the slides."

Focusing on the art of composing presentations will help you add tremendous substance to your personal style. This skill set will also help you to identify and avoid pitfalls common to a relaxed delivery style, such as the following:

- Going over time, which can frustrate your audience and dilute your overall impact

- Going off on tangents, which can be fun to do but can make it hard for your audience to follow and often obscure your most important points

This book provides tools and techniques to help you write (and then deliver) well-composed presentations, in your own personal style.

Are you a nervous presenter?

Take heart! When you focus your energy on composing your presentations, it takes your attention away from yourself and puts your focus where 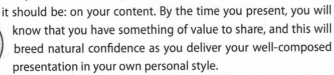 it should be: on your content. By the time you present, you will know that you have something of value to share, and this will breed natural confidence as you deliver your well-composed presentation in your own personal style.

COMPOSING A PRESENTATION = COMPOSING A SONG ·

If there's a similarity between the act of presenting and the act of singing, then we can also draw the comparison between the act of composing a presentation and the act of composing a song.

Now, you might be thinking, *Hold on a second! Are we saying that writing a good presentation takes as much creativity, inspiration, and time as it does to write an actual song? That makes it sound hard!*

Actually, yes. That's exactly what I'm saying!

Writing captivating presentations is an art, which takes skill, creativity, and time.

However, just like the art of songwriting, it *can* be learned. And, like anything else, it's not too hard when you know how to do it.

Have you ever given thought to your personal presentation-writing approach? For example, do you follow a process or a certain methodology? Have you developed any "hacks" to expedite your writing process? When you start working on a new presentation, do you know exactly where to begin and which activities you should begin to schedule? Or do you feel stressed and wait until the last minute?

This book will help you find good answers to all of these questions. We'll cover methods, rules to follow, hacks to try, ideas to play with, and tools to use that will help you develop and solidify your own personal writing style.

Taking the time to develop your presentation-writing style is a wise investment. When you are excited to share something that you've created, you will shine brightly every time you deliver a presentation, which will help you to develop a reputation as an excellent presenter. This, in turn, can make you stand out in your career. The concepts in this book will help you tackle every presentation you write with confidence.

So, if writing a presentation is like writing a song, let's ask a simple question to get started: If you wanted to learn the art of songwriting, where would you start?

Any experienced songwriter would tell you that you'd need to understand some essential songwriting concepts:

1. **Song theory:** The fundamental principles and ideas present in the music genre you want to write

2. **Song structure:** The common structural elements present in songs of your chosen genre

3. **Songwriting process:** Methods for developing your lyrics and melodies

Since we are comparing presentation writing to songwriting, we will use these same concepts as they relate to presentations:

- In Section 1, we'll focus on *presentation theory* and explore the essential principles and ideas present within the types of presentations many people aspire to write.

- In Section 2, we'll explore the *structure of presentations* and review a tried-and-tested framework you can use for your own presentations.

- In Section 3, we'll do a deep dive into the *presentation-writing process*, where we will explore a step-by-step method for creating melodious words for your presentations.

When exactly does one "take the stage"?

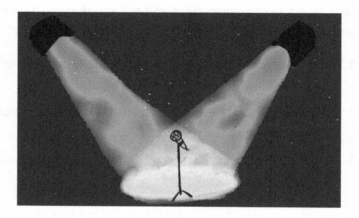

Any time you are asked to prepare something to say to an audience, you are delivering a presentation. I know that might sound obvious, but it's not. Obviously, there are occasions with a big fat "this is an important presentation" label on them, perhaps at a company-wide meeting, at a conference, or at an event, maybe even as the maid of honor or the best man in your best friend's wedding.

For a moment to qualify as a presentation, the audience doesn't have to be thousands of people sitting in chairs while you take the stage. The audience could be just one person, perhaps your boss, who wants to hear your idea. It could be a department meeting where you are asked to update the team on progress or share your plans. Whenever you have the occasion to present to one person or a thousand, you should view it as an opportunity to present something of value and leave a deep impression with your audience.

The principles in this book apply to every presentation scenario, regardless of the number of people you'll be talking to.

When you write your own material, you can present in your own style

When you observe a dynamic, vivacious presenter, it's easy to think, *I wish I was more like that!* While it's great to be inspired by others, try to focus on being yourself rather than someone else.

Here's what I mean: I think that U2's Bono is an incredible front man. U2 concerts are a spectacle to behold as Bono owns the stage and works the crowd like a master puppeteer.

I also happen to really enjoy the singer Jewel (I have a signed book of her poetry—don't tell anyone). The last time I saw Jewel perform live, she sat on a stool, played her songs, and told a few stories in between—it was an excellent, enjoyable evening.

However, it would be weird for Jewel to try to emulate Bono's

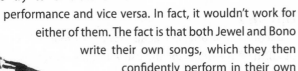

performance and vice versa. In fact, it wouldn't work for either of them. The fact is that both Jewel and Bono write their own songs, which they then confidently perform in their own unique style.

Similarly, when you write presentations that you are proud of, you can feel confident in your material and can then focus on delivering them in your own personal style.

Help! I have a presentation coming up, my slides are very wordy, and I don't have time to read and apply this book before I present!

If you have a wordy, wordy, wordy slide deck, here are two quick-fix options for you:

Option 1

Do these steps in order, as they can dramatically improve the effectiveness of your slides:

Step 1: Reduce your paragraphs to sentences.

Step 2: Reduce your sentences to bullet points.

Step 3: Replace your bullet points with icons, images, or diagrams. (See Section 3 for examples.)

Even if you only have time for Steps 1 and 2, at the very least, your slides will be easier to look at and digest.

Option 2

If you don't have any time at all to work on your slide deck, this is my top tip: Turn off the projector and use your slides as notes.

So many presentations would be exponentially better if nothing was projected. The only thing that is accomplished when you project wordy slides is that you distract your audience from what you are saying and overwhelm them.

If you have ever tried reading something while someone is talking to you (shout out to my beautiful kids . . . sorry!!), you know that it's *really* hard to read and listen at the same time.

When you project words on a screen, your audience will start reading what's up there, whether you want them to or not. They'll also read the words on the slides faster than you can read them aloud. By simply turning off the projector, your audience will listen to you much more attentively, and you won't have to feel self-conscious that your slides aren't pretty.

If you want to improve your presentations before you have finished reading this book, just use this hack: Use your existing slides as notes but don't project them.

Try it!

SECTION 1:
THE AMMMAZING
PRESENTATION THEORY

—

THE ESSENTIAL PRINCIPLES, IDEAS, AND CONCEPTS BEHIND THE VERY BEST PRESENTATIONS

INTRODUCING THE AMMMAZING PRESENTATION THEORY

IF YOU WERE GOING TO write an actual song, first you'd have to figure out what kind of song you wanted to write. There are many musical styles out there: pop, rock, jazz, folk, classical, electronic, punk . . . the list goes on and on and on.

I'd hazard a guess that you'd want to write songs in your favorite genre of music. In other words, you'd write a song that you yourself would like to hear.

This is a great way to think about your presentations: Apply the golden rule to "deliver presentations to others that you would have them deliver to you."

Here's a caveat, though: In the slight chance that you are a big fan of acid jazz or psychedelic black metal—yes, that's an actual genre—the whole point of this analogy is that your goal should be to write something that your *audience* really enjoys listening to.

Let's use the term "radio friendly" as our goal. This still leaves a lot of room for your own personal taste, and this expression captures the idea that our goal is to write something with mass appeal. One definition for "radio friendly" regarding songs is "suitable for the mainstream; appealing to popular taste, free from profanity." I'm sure you would agree that these are all excellent things to strive for in our presentations!

With that in mind, how do you write a presentation that is enjoyable to listen to, easy on the ear, and engaging?

You simply have to make your presentation *aMMMazing!*

WHAT IS AN AMMMAZING PRESENTATION?

First of all, that's not a typo!

The three *M*s in "aMMMazing" represent the three hallmarks of exceptional presentations: *meaningful, memorable,* and *motivational.* A truly great presentation is all three of these things.

The three *M*s mean that we are proactively involving the audience in multiple ways. We are trying to reach their heart by creating something meaningful for them. We are trying to involve their brain by structuring and presenting our information in a way that will make it memorable. We are also trying to influence our listeners' actions as we strive to motivate them.

If you think this is all fluff, think about the opposite of the three *M*s. Do you want your presentation to be meaningless, forgettable, and unable to incite any positive action whatsoever? Of course not! In fact, we could say that the opposite of an aMM-Mazing presentation is a **BAD** presentation: **B**oring **A**nd **D**ull. BAD presentations are forgettable because they don't connect with the audience and often overwhelm the listeners with too much information, audibly and visually.

DON'T WRITE BAD PRESENTATIONS!

It must be said that no one who prepares or delivers a presentation ever intends for it to be boring and dull. The unfortunate fact is, though, many presentations we hear (and perhaps have delivered ourselves) have come across this way. When the information is disorganized, when your eyes and ears are overwhelmed with too many words, and when you didn't quite catch *why* the information was important to you, that's where we experience the opposite of the three *M*'s.

At this point, you might be thinking, *Whoa there! The presentations I normally deliver are just informational. All this talk of affecting feelings, coming up with memorable points, and wanting my audience to be motivated doesn't apply to me.* It's true that some presentations must contain a lot of information and maybe the purpose is simply to update your listeners, but the three *M*'s apply to all presentations, not just keynotes or when you are on a big stage.

Perhaps you are presenting financial updates or information from spreadsheets to another department. Do you want your listeners to understand why the information matters to them? Do you want them to remember at least something after you present? Is there a reason why you are sharing the information with them? I'm certain that the answer to at least one of these questions is yes.

If not, then one may wonder why you are presenting the information in the first place.

Given that people listen to presentations with their ears and listen to songs with the same ears, just for fun let's apply the three *M*'s to both to see how these same concepts apply in our analogy. Next, let's discuss each *M* in turn to explore how to make your presentations meaningful, memorable, and motivational.

Body parts involved (besides ears)	The *M*	Songs	Presentations
	Meaningful	Great songs are *meaningful* to you. They reach a deeper part of you, make you feel something: happy, sad, reflective, or angry (if you are into psychedelic black metal).	Captivating presentations are *meaningful* to you. They reach your heart and make you feel or think differently about something.
	Memorable	Great songs are *memorable*. They have catchy melodies, hooks, riffs, and lyrics that stick in your mind.	Captivating presentations are *memorable*. They are easy to follow and contain thoughts that we will remember, sometimes for a long time.
	Motivational	Great songs *motivate* you. They make you want to do something: tap your feet, tap your fingers on the steering wheel, sing along, dance, cry, or tell that person how you really feel about them before it's too late.	Captivating presentations *motivate* you. They inspire you to take action, to do something different than you did before, to make a decision, or to tell that person how you really feel about them before it's too late (OK, I was just joking with that last one, unless it's a presentation about relationships).

1

THE FIRST *M*: MEANINGFUL

HOW DO WE ENSURE THAT our presentations are meaningful to our audience? Here's the principle we should keep in mind whenever we have a new presentation to create: Ask questions first, create content later. It should be "ready, aim, fire!" instead of "ready, fire, aim."

READY, AIM, <u>FIRE</u>!　　　　READY, <u>FIRE</u>, AIM!

So, what questions should you ask? I have been involved in many presentation brainstorming sessions over the years. Without any guidance, the brainstorming sessions usually revolve around what the presenter wants to say. We need to shift the conversation to what the audience needs to hear.

Before we go any further, let's take a little quiz.

Question: When I start working on a new presentation, the first thing I am most likely to do is

    a. Open a slideware application and start typing.

    b. Grab a pen and paper.

    c. Ask questions.

If you answered A, put down the laptop and step away from the slides. This is the hardest path to creating an aMMMazing presentation. Please choose another answer. Section 3: The JAM Session Writing Process will go into detail as to why this is not the best answer.

If you answered B, this is much better than answer A. This might sound foreign in our digital age, and we'll expand on this concept later on. But this is still not the best response.

If you answered C, fantastic! Your head is in the right place. Before starting work on any presentation, it is essential that you first ask some key questions. Not only will this ultimately expedite the creation of your presentation, it is essential if you want your presentation to be meaningful to your audience. Want to learn three essential questions that will forever improve your presentations? Read on!

There are three simple (but essential) questions to ask that will help you figure out what your audience wants to hear. These may sound basic, but you must know the answers to them if you want your presentation to be meaningful.

TIP! Write down the answers to these questions because they will help you figure out the most meaningful information to include.

1. Who is my audience? _____

2. What do they care about? _____

3. What do I want them to do? _____

The answers to these questions help you to channel your thought process to include the right things in your presentation. Let's examine these essential questions one at a time. Once you have the answer to each question, *write it down.*

1. Who is my audience?

I can't even count the number of times that I've been deep into a brainstorming session when someone will say, "Oh, by the way, who's the audience?" and then we find that the answer changes the direction of our thinking. Sometimes the answer to that question is obvious, but it also can be surprising. For example, in one brainstorming session for a keynote presentation, the assumption was that the audience mostly consisted of longtime attendees of the event. After drilling into the registrants, we discovered that most were first-time attendees. This had a significant impact on the material that we decided to include.

Notice that the question is "Who is my audience?" instead of "Who is in the room?" Sometimes the answers to these questions are the same, but sometimes they are not. For example, there may be a group of executives around a board table, but the audience you are *really* targeting is your boss and your CEO. Therefore, you should tailor what you are saying to them specifically.

On other occasions, there is a massive room full of people at a conference. You can't possibly create one presentation that is going to be meaningful for every single individual, but you can appeal to a majority if you are able to collectively describe the attendees as a group. So, you would need to give some thought as to who they are as a group and why they are there.

Plenty of templates out there can help you identify and analyze who is in your audience. Some of these tools are simple and useful, but some include *way* too much detail for most presentations. For example, some tools suggest that you find out the ratio of men versus women, age range, religion, ethnicity, and other personal details—there would have to be a very good reason to find out details like this. I find that simply defining who your target audience is, in general terms, is good enough.

Here are some examples, where I've defined the audiences at conferences where I've presented:

- Thousand-plus marketing professionals who have paid to learn best practices and new ideas

- Prospective clients (and some competitors) who don't yet fully understand the value of my company's offerings

- Fifteen hundred-plus existing customers in a variety of roles—from end users to executives

Once you've determined who your audience is, then you need to figure out the answer to the second question.

2. What do they care about?

If you want to make sure that your presentation is meaningful to your audience, you must try to answer this question the best you can. Let's look at this list of common presentation scenarios and consider some reasonable high-level questions to help you contemplate what these audiences may care about.

- **Pitching your product or service to a prospect**
  - What does your prospect care more about?
    - **a.** Your company and products
    - **b.** Solving their own business challenges and improving their bottom line
- **Presenting an idea to your boss**
  - What does your boss care more about?
    - **a.** The details of how you are going to implement your idea
    - **b.** How this idea will improve her department (and make her look good to her boss)
- **Speaking at a conference**
  - What do the attendees care more about?
    - **a.** Your company history and competitive differentiators
    - **b.** Learning new ideas and ways of doing something
- **Presenting a team overview at a company meeting**
  - What do these employees care more about?

    a. Your team's organizational structure

    b. How your department and function can help them in their jobs

- **Presenting a financial update to all employees**
  - What do the majority of your employees care about?

    a. Company profit margins

    b. Job stability, benefits, and their own prospect of getting a raise

Of course, these are all generalized, but hopefully, these questions and the *B* answers illustrate the point. Figuring out what your audience cares about (and what they don't care about) can help you fundamentally shape what you choose to include and how you choose to frame it. In that last example, impressive company profit margins are certainly an important thing to communicate, but the message will be stronger if you can draw a direct correlation to how it benefits the people who are working so hard, rather than just the absent shareholders.

You may also want to take this one step further and ask about the sentiment of the people in the room because this often determines what they care about at that moment. For example, let's say you are going to talk to an existing customer and are trying to convince them to buy more from you. Are they happy with your relationship? Are they angry over something that doesn't work as expected? Are they disappointed in a recent interaction? Knowing this level of detail can make the difference as you frame your information in a way that adds meaning for them.

After we've figured out who we are talking to, next we ask my favorite question of all.

3. What do I want them to do?

Notice that it's not "what do I want them to *know*" but "what do I want them to *do*."

Every single time I pose this question to someone during a brainstorming session, the immediate response is . . . silence.

The reason for the silence is that the answer to this question is not always obvious.

After the silence, the most common response is "Well, I don't want them to *do* anything. I just want them to listen."

My response to that is "If your audience will not do anything different as a result of your presentation, what was the point of talking?" I know that's kind of annoying to hear, but it's worth thinking about.

Here are some examples of goals or actions that you might have in mind for your audience:

- To buy what you are selling (an idea, product, or service)
- To agree to act on your idea
- To stop doing something
- To appreciate something that they didn't previously
- To upgrade to a new version
- To engage with your team and know how to do it
- To increase their confidence in you, your team, or your company
- To donate time, energy, or money

PICK A VERB, ANY VERB

So basically, pick a verb that you want your audience to do, and craft a sentence around it. That is the goal of your presentation. This can serve as your "true north" when deciding what you should include. And by the way, once you have written down the goal of your presentation, it's worth revisiting as you go through the brainstorming and writing process. Presentations often suffer from "presentation creep," where there are so many good ideas that you want to cram them all in. Keeping the goal for your audience firmly in mind will help you select the best ideas, cut out unnecessary content, and resist the temptation to throw in additional details not aligned to your goal.

THE THREE ESSENTIAL QUESTIONS RESULT IN SOMETHING GAME-CHANGING

If you ask these three essential questions every time you write a presentation, you'll quickly realize something monumentally important: *The answers will be different every time you present!* Each audience is unique and has unique cares. And based on these factors, your intended goal for them might vary too. This means that the information you include in your presentation should be tailored to your audience, every time. That is really worth thinking about.

There is no such thing as a "stock" presentation. Let me rephrase that. There is no such thing as a stock presentation that will work for all audiences and situations. Even if you have a corporate fact sheet or slide deck where you pull standard content from, if you want to make your presentation meaningful to your audience, you must *always* tailor your presentation to them.

THE CORPORATE DISEASE

Speaking of stock slide decks, let's look at why presentations should be tailored to your audience every time you present, instead of grabbing a stock deck from a shelf and just talking through it. This is something that I like to call the "corporate disease" of all presentation formats.

I am no conspiracy theorist, but I do think that there must have been a secret society of powerfully boring people that got together back in the early '80s. This cabal decided to create the most mind-numbing of all presentation formats they could think of, then secretly seeded it throughout corporations around the world. For the past forty years, organizations have adopted this format en masse and have continued to churn out corporate presentations accordingly.

*Society of Really Rotten Yarns NOT Society of Remarkably Riveting Yaks

Here is the format of the corporate disease presentation:

The Corporate Disease Agenda

- **Our History**
  - Background of our company
  - Where we are based
  - Number of employees
  - Partnership status with other vendors
- **Our Company Values**
  - They are just like yours!
- **Our Obligatory Logo Slide** of Impressive Companies We've Worked With
- **Our Placement on Analyst Reports**
- **Our Products or Services**
- **Our Demo** (If There's Time!)

I know that you've seen this format. You have probably delivered this format. And maybe, by some weird chance, you created a slide deck in this format for a company, and now you are wondering how you got infected by the corporate disease.

Here's when I first noticed that this was a problem: A few years ago, I had the opportunity to participate in a product pitch night in Cleveland, Ohio. Ten local companies had the opportunity to deliver a ten-minute pitch of their products and services to a group of business owners and executives. At the end of the event, the attendees would vote on a variety of categories related to the pitch.

Seven out of the ten pitches followed this exact format. What completely blew my mind was that, even though all of the companies offered unique products and services, all of their presentations were so similar that it was even hard to differentiate one company from another!

All companies had a founding date and were proud of where they were from. All of them had stellar core values. All of them had analyst recognition (with their company shown as a dot on a quadrant, wave, or report). All seven of these near-identical pitches didn't even get to the problems they solved or even what they did until the very end of their ten-minute slot. And even then, most of them either ran out of time or didn't fully explain the value! These presenters had a full ten minutes to pitch the value of their products (which is plenty of time to make a great pitch), but for some inexplicable reason, they opted to include so much irrelevant corporate information that the value of their products was lost.

IDENTICAL   UNIQUE

These presenters did not ask or answer the three essential questions. If they had, they never would have delivered that content to that audience because it just wasn't relevant or what the night was actually about. It's not a stretch to imagine that this is the exact same deck that these companies use when pitching their products and solutions to prospects.

Walking away from this event, I realized something that every sales organization should take to heart: If this presentation format makes it almost impossible to differentiate between companies that offer completely different products, imagine how difficult it makes it for you to differentiate your company from your competitors who solve the exact same problems you do!

Here's another observation about why this format is ineffective: The real problem isn't just that everyone delivers the same outline; the real problem is who the presentation is focused on. Look back at the first word of each major bullet point in the corporate disease agenda. You probably didn't pick up on it at first, but the first word in each of these points is "our." It's problematic when the focus of the information is on the presenter rather than on the audience. The corporate disease outline is focused on the company that is delivering the presentation, not on the needs of the people in the audience and what they care about.

This is not to say that your company's history, partnership status, and other successes are totally irrelevant. I'm also not saying that you should throw away your corporate slide deck. It's all about context, the order of the information, and when this information is the headline or when it's supporting material. The presentation should be more about your audience than about yourself.

Imagine being invited out on a first date and talking about yourself for the first forty-five minutes, trying to convince your date they did the right thing by asking you out. I'm no romantic guru, but I'm not sure a second date would be forthcoming.

In the scenario of pitching to a prospect, remember this: Your prospect already knows (and likes) enough about your company to have invited you along to pitch your solution in the first place.

To illustrate the point, let's stick with our prospect-pitching scenario in a sales situation and revisit the three essential questions in that context.

1. Who is the audience?

    a. Answer: Perhaps the chief technology officer, CEO, or another key decision-maker

2. What do they care about?

    b. Answer: Probably solving their problems and improving their bottom line

3. What do I want them to do?

    c. Answer: Get the best solution to their challenges (which is what we are offering!)

Now, go back and examine the content from the standard corporate disease pitch deck. When you look at this presentation scenario, is your history, core values, analyst recognition, and product breadth and depth the most important information to begin with? Probably not. What is relevant is how you can uniquely solve their challenges and help your prospect achieve their goals— so why not start with that?

Now we can get back to our songwriting analogy with all of this in mind. If you were to start writing a song for someone special, would you include lots of lyrics about yourself or lots of lyrics meaningful to them? The answer is fairly obvious!

When you are writing a presentation, you are writing it for your audience, so make it about them.

Are you in sales? Consider this! When you show up to deliver a pitch, your prospect is likely going to hear pitches from several of your competitors. Let's assume that your competitors will show up and deliver the corporate disease format. They will all end up sounding exactly the same to your prospect. That's where your presentation itself can become one of your greatest differentiators (if you follow the steps in this book!).

2

THE SECOND *M*: MEMORABLE

NOW THAT WE KNOW HOW to narrow our information down to the most meaningful content, let's consider the second *M*. How do you make sure that your presentation is *memorable*—that your audience will remember your key points?

If you want to write memorable presentations, the first thing you need to embrace is this reality: *Your audience will not remember everything that you say.*

Without getting into the science of it, think back to the last presentation you heard. Unless you have a photographic or eidetic memory, you likely do not remember every single word that the presenter said. If you think really hard, you might be able to remember a few of the things the presenter said. You might also remember that you were hungry, that the room was cold, or that the slides were difficult to read. Or you might struggle to remember it at all.

Embracing the reality that your audience will, at best, only remember a few things about your presentation in the minutes, hours, and days following it is one of the most liberating concepts of all when it comes to writing presentations. Why? Because once you embrace this concept, you can take control of it.

Through this revelation, you will realize that adding specific memory-aiding techniques to your presentation is a really good idea. We are going to cover three of those techniques that will help your audience remember what you want them to remember, rather than leaving it to chance.

These are "the rule of three," mnemonics, and repetition.

THE RULE OF THREE

If you found yourself on fire, you wouldn't have a lot of time to do a Google search for what to do. Instead, you would "stop, drop, and roll."

You may not remember that it was Dick Van Dyke who made this phrase famous in an educational campaign in the '70s (did a lot of people spontaneously combust back then?), but you'll be glad he used the rule of three when he promoted this phrase because our brains find it very easy to remember things in threes. Even dry data like phone numbers are grouped into threes to make them easier to remember (which was handy when we needed to remember phone numbers).

Take a moment to think about three-word phrases that you know and where they are used. Can you finish these phrases?

* **In advertising:** A Mars a day helps you work, rest . . .
* **In literature:** Friends, Romans . . .

- **In sandwiches**: Bacon, lettuce . . .

Think about stories and rhymes that have been passed on by word of mouth for generations: Goldilocks and her three fluffy companions, the three little pigs, and the three billy goats gruff. If you have ever sat down with a kid and told them any of these tales from memory, you have experienced the weird phenomenon that not only is your brain able to recall the three main characters, but it is also able to fill in a remarkable amount of detail around them, even if you haven't read or heard the story yourself in years.

A plethora of articles extol the benefits of the rule of three, proving that it works with even more examples and interesting theories as to *why* our brains easily latch on to things in threes, so I won't belabor it here. The point is that it is a very powerful memory aid, it works, and if we want people to remember what we've been talking about, we should use it.

In fact, once you connect the dots between the rule of three and the fact that your audience will only remember a few things you say, you can use this to your advantage. You can highlight the three things that you want them to remember within your presentation.

While there's a lot of content saying that you should use the rule of three, there's not as much advice for how to do it. It's a classic case of "easier said than done."

So how do you do it? As shown in the previous examples, one obvious way is to coin a three-part phrase that everyone will remember. If you can do that, that's great! However, there's one specific application of the rule of three that I highly recommend, and it's perhaps the most practical application of the rule of three in presenting. I have made the following rule about the rule of three for the presentations I write: *Always have exactly three items on the agenda. No more, no less.*

To do this, it means that you have to arrange all of your material into three topics, headings, or main points. When you are previewing your agenda during your introduction, your slide might look something like this:

Your immediate reaction might be "That will never work for my presentations because I usually need to cover way more than three things." This doesn't mean that you can only cover three points or that it restricts you from covering everything you want to (assuming you've already selected only the most meaningful information). It does, however, require you to spend some time brainstorming, arranging, and rearranging your ideas until you can organize them into three simple, *memorable,* and digestible topics. This is one of the best ways to make your information appealingly simple.

That might sound challenging, but I promise that it is one of the secrets to delivering memorable presentations. By holding fast to the three-point-agenda rule, I find that it helps me, as the presenter, to organize my thoughts and find patterns and relationships within my information that I had not previously recognized.

Having a three-point agenda may seem like an extreme recommendation, but who really brims with anticipation when a presenter shows an agenda with more points on it than one can even read through? It's a rough place to start if your audience feels overwhelmed before you've even begun.

When you simplify your information into three main topics, it makes it easy for you, as the presenter, to introduce your content, and it makes it really simple for your listeners to absorb and anticipate what you will be saying.

There's another added benefit: It makes it easy for you, as the presenter, to remember what you are going to cover.

Imagine you have a pending presentation, and someone says to you, "What's your presentation about?" This is an easy question to answer because you'll just tell them your topic. But then, what if they say, "That sounds interesting. What are you going to say about it?" Can you summarize the key points of a presentation you are about to deliver without reaching for your slide deck?

Confession Time!

I once delivered a presentation about the benefits of a software application I had been learning (Citrix remote desktop, in case you are interested). In my original presentation, I had so many agenda items that I had to split my agenda over two slides! A two-slide agenda! Can you even imagine!? After realizing that the best presentations use the rule of three, rather than trying to spread my agenda over two slides, I made it my mission to rework it into three points. This is what I ended up with:

1. The Benefits of Citrix

continued

2. How Citrix Works

3. Troubleshooting Citrix Issues

I didn't reduce the actual content, but I did reorganize it significantly. As I reorganized my information, I started to realize that in my first version I had been regularly touching on ideas related to benefits, how it works, and troubleshooting, but they were scattered throughout my whole presentation. When I consolidated all similar ideas and presented them together, my presentation was much better. Not only was the information much clearer for my audience, the result was much more satisfying for me to deliver.

If you have already arranged your information into three topics, you will find it surprisingly easy to recall your key ideas or sections and preview your presentation off the top of your mind. You will find that you can recall a remarkable amount of the detail around your three ideas. If you have not spent the time to do this and have a ten-part agenda, you will find that it is really hard to articulate, or even call to mind, your main ideas.

Here's the point: If you cannot call to mind a brief synopsis of your presentation (without scrolling through your slide deck to conjure up some key points) before you present, how on earth can you expect your audience to remember your key points after you've talked?

When you take the time to arrange your material into three sections, ideas, or main points, what you are really doing is spending valuable time simplifying your message so that your audience can absorb and remember it. We will cover tips and techniques for how to distill your information into three key ideas in Section 3, but for now, simply bear in mind that a three-point agenda is a rule that we will apply from here on.

Before we examine our next memory aid technique, I will address three common objections to using a three-point agenda.

OBJECTION 1: I NEED MORE THAN THREE AGENDA POINTS FOR MY MEETING!

You might be thinking about meeting agendas that you've built that include breaks, lunch, tours, several presentations, time for questions and answers, and more. If you are, then you are probably thinking that I'm crazy in saying that your presentation should only have three items on it.

There's a difference between a meeting agenda and a presentation agenda. Your meeting agenda can have as many items as you need, but each distinct presentation should have a simple three-item agenda, like this:

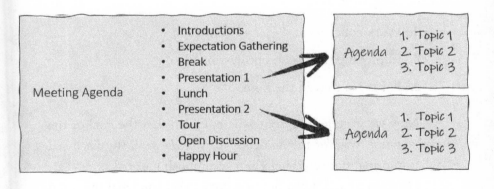

The meeting agenda lays out how the time will be spent during the meeting. When the individual presenters take the stage to present, their presentation agendas should be arranged around their three key ideas, aligned to the goal of their individual sessions.

OBJECTION 2: I CANNOT POSSIBLY REDUCE MY INFORMATION TO THREE POINTS!

Someone once approached me and said, "I hear what you are saying about the rule of three and I want to apply it, except that
I'm about to deliver a presentation on Stephen Covey's book *The
7 Habits of Highly Effective People*. How do I explain the seven
habits if I can only have three main points?" This, as you have
probably deduced, was a very good question!

So, I decided to ask a series of questions. Can you guess which
ones? I asked him—

1. Who is your audience?
2. What do they care about?
3. What do you want them to do?

Here were his answers:

1. Work colleagues
2. Improving themselves professionally
3. For them to read the book

Now we were getting somewhere! Given that the goal of the
presentation was for the audience to *read the book*, we discussed
what information would help him accomplish his goal.

He realized that it was not necessary to explain what the seven
habits even were! He ended up focusing his presentation on making
a compelling case for people to *read the book*. After some brainstorming and applying the methodologies we'll cover in Section 3,
we came up with this simple agenda for his presentation:

1. Why the seven habits matter

2. Results from applying them

3. Where to learn more (read the book!)

Applying the rule of three saved him (and his audience) from the path he was going down, which was trying to cram all the actual seven habits into ten minutes.

Here's the point: Even the most perplexing of topics can be distilled into three main points if you ask yourself the three essential questions and build a presentation to help you meet your goal.

OBJECTION 3: IT SOUNDS HARD, SO I'LL JUST IGNORE IT

If this is your objection, remember this: *It's called a rule for a reason.*

You can try to ignore the rule of three and pretend it doesn't exist, but the rule of three is a bit like gravity; you can't escape it, no matter how hard you try.

You have probably heard the somewhat clichéd phrase "blood, sweat, and tears" before. This phrase, coined by Winston Churchill, is often used when describing the effort involved in accomplishing a difficult task. Did you know, though, that Churchill actually said, "blood, sweat, *toil,* and tears"? The rule of three left the somewhat unnecessary word toil behind.

Not only do we remember things better grouped into threes, but our own brain also uses the rule of three to selectively remember the most important points. Who knows if the Canadian-American jazz-rock band Blood, Sweat & Tears knew they were influenced by the rule of three? But one thing's for sure: A band name of Blood, Sweat, Toil & Tears is just not as catchy.

Here's one more example. I mentioned the three little pigs earlier. If you had to tell a little kid that story right now, I'm betting that you could, even if you hadn't heard it or read it in years. There were three pigs, and each one built a house out of a different material: straw, wood, and brick, respectively. The big bad wolf said to each pig, "I'm going to huff and puff and blow your house down." This story is riddled with threes, which is why it's easy to remember.

THREE PIGS, THREE BUILDINGS, THREE WORDS

Did you remember, however, that prior to the wolf climbing down the chimney and getting boiled alive (how graphic!), there's a whole subplot where the wolf coaxes the last little piggy out of his brick house three times? Eventually, the little piggy hides in a butter churn, then proceeds to roll down a hill and totally freak the wolf out, which is what causes him to climb down the chimney and meet his grisly end! Maybe you recall those scenes, but I had no idea until I bought the storybook and found these details as I read it to my son! Either my parents didn't remember that part when they told the story to me, or I forgot it somewhere along the way. In fact, many printed and online versions of this story omit these details. These seem to be left on the cutting room floor of people's memory. Why? Maybe because they were unnecessary to the overall point of the story? I'll attribute this to the rule of three.

The rule of three is an excellent principle to help you simplify and distill your key ideas as much as possible. You can try to ignore it, but you can't avoid it. People will only remember a few things that you said. The best thing to do is embrace this fact and start organizing your information into three points.

But there are still other techniques to help your audience remember important content along with the rule of three.

MNEMONICS

Mnemonics is the technique of using memory aids such as rhymes, poems, acronyms, acrostics, images, and other mental association concepts to help remember complex things. These mnemonic devices can stick in your mind for years to come.

Coming back to our songwriting analogy for a second, there's a direct relationship between songs and mnemonics. For example, many children learn the "ABC" song, which is not really a song at all. It's just the alphabet put to the tune of "Twinkle, Twinkle, Little Star." The melody aids the memory.

Similarly, many songs that you hear include a hook. This might be a highly recognizable phrase, a melody, or a riff that catches your ear and gets stuck in your head. Here are some famous examples:

- The opening piano riff in "Clocks" by Coldplay

- The strings in the song "Bitter Sweet Symphony" by the Verve (a hook they found so catchy they borrowed it from the Rolling Stones)

- The bass groove in "Seven Nation Army" by The White Stripes, which is so catchy that football fans (a.k.a. soccer fans!) spontaneously chant this throughout the globe

These song elements catch your ear and are often repeated a few times throughout the song, therefore becoming memorable.

What is the counterpart in presentations? Here are some examples of a hook in a presentation:

- Analogies

- Quotes from a famous person or a customer

- Stories or anecdotes

- Customer case studies

- Statistics

- Rhetorical questions

- News articles

When you include one or more carefully chosen elements like these, they can create a deeper and more memorable impression than just your raw information alone.

Story Time!

I once created a presentation to help employees get on board with some large organizational changes that were coming. I wove in an analogy that illustrated the positive effects that can happen when organizations drive market changes rather than react to them. One of the leaders involved in driving the organizational change told me, "You need to get rid of the analogy and get straight to the details of what's changing—that's what's most important." Unfortunately (or should I say, fortunately), this conversation happened the day before I was due to deliver the presentation, and I had already created, rehearsed, and timed the entire thing.

As I was planning on delivering the presentation several times to a variety of departments over a period of a few weeks, I proceeded with the presentation as planned on its first airing. I decided that I would make changes (if necessary) based on the response.

Afterward, one of the people in the audience said to me, "I knew *what* was changing in our organization, but I never really understood *why* we were going through all this change. Your analogy really helped me grasp it." Interestingly, the person who said this was a model example of the audience we were trying to target.

The point is that sometimes a well-chosen analogy or story can help to communicate broader or more impactful ideas than the information alone. Even years later, people mentioned that same presentation to me, referring to it by the analogy I used.

Your "hook" might ultimately help you make a deeper and more memorable impression than just the details of the topic at hand.

Another example of a memory aid technique is acrostics. For example, how do you recall the order of the points on a compass? Personally, I Never Eat Shredded Wheat.

A well-known business example is SMART goals. Without turning to Google (I promise), I grabbed a pen and paper and jotted down these words from memory: Specific, Measurable, Actionable, Realistic, and Time-Based. A quick Google search to validate my memory revealed a slight difference: Specific, Measurable, *Achievable, Relevant*, and Time-Bound. Even with this slight discrepancy, I'd argue that this technique still worked amazingly well. I learned these definitions from a single presentation several years ago. While the words in my memory were slightly different, the general concept and ideas stuck in my mind. I'd consider this a win considering all of the presentations that I've heard and not remembered anything from in the last decade!

Let's go back to the presentation on *The 7 Habits of Highly Effective People*. Let's say that the presenter had an hour to speak on the topic rather than ten minutes. Let's assume that his goal changed (given the time allowed) from wanting the audience to read the book to learning the seven habits. I would still insist on a three-part agenda for the presentation, and it might look something like this now:

1. Why the seven habits matter

2. What are the seven habits?

3. How to apply them

In this structure, the presenter would explain the seven habits one by one during the second topic. But what if he wanted to help his audience to remember them? For reference, here are Stephen Covey's seven habits:[2]

1. Be proactive.

2. Begin with the end in mind.

3. Put first things first.

4. Think win-win.

5. Seek first to understand, then to be understood.

6. Synergize.

7. Sharpen the saw.

This is a big list and therefore hard to remember. Also, you can't boil them down to three because there are literally seven of them! How could a presenter help an audience remember all seven? The presenter could identify the main word from each habit and then create a mnemonic as a fun memory aid, as follows:

People Enjoy Feeling Wise Using Stephen's Saw

---

2   Stephen R. Covey, *The 7 Habits of Highly Effective People: Powerful Lessons in Personal Change* (New York: Free Press, 2004).

This sentence is easier to remember than the seven points alone and can help someone remember the first letter of the key word within each of the seven points in order. Our brains are amazing tools because often, with the simple trigger of one letter, we can recall the rest of the detail that was otherwise buried in the deepest recesses of our minds.

Obviously, these take some time to think through, but they can be fun to create and share, and can help your content stick in people's minds.

REPETITION

If the rule of three and mnemonics can help you create memorable content, then the concept of repetition is like the hammer that can drive these same points home.

Just as you rarely drive a nail home with one hit of a hammer, the concept of repetition means that you need to hit on your key ideas at least a few times throughout your presentation. There's a Latin proverb that says, "Repetition is the mother of all learning." I don't think anyone would argue with that.

But what things should you repeat throughout your presentation? While repetition is the easiest of all the memory aids to apply, we have purposefully added it at the end of this chapter on making your presentation memorable, because we've now identified some of the things that you should repeat.

If you have identified your three key ideas, come up with a hook, and created some mnemonics to really make them stick in people's minds, you should repeat these throughout your presentation.

Have you ever heard the adage "Tell them what you are going to tell them, tell them, and tell them what you told them"? This concept applies as much today as it did when the words were first recorded in the early 1900s. It's the simple concept of "introduce the idea, explain the idea, summarize the idea." I'll show how you can build this concept into the structure of your presentation in Section 2. This simple advice is very interesting because the phrase itself incorporates the rule of three and repetition (and is therefore easy to remember), and if you apply it, you will incorporate the rule of three and repetition in your own presentations. It's a magic trick for presentations!

> Ye canny repeat yer key ideas if ye dinny ken them yersel'!

However, to apply this repetition technique successfully, you have to apply the three-point-agenda rule and simplify your information into a few memorable, repeatable topics. It's difficult to introduce a ten-part agenda, explain it, and then summarize it at the end.

To wrap up this concept for now, along with the

Latin proverb, I thought I'd include a modern-day Scottish proverb: "Ye canny repeat yer key ideas if ye dinny ken them yersel'."*

Translation: "You cannot repeat your key ideas if you don't know them yourself."

*I'm Scottish and I just wrote it, so that counts as modern-day Scottish, right?

3

THE THIRD *M*:
MOTIVATIONAL

THIS LAST *M* IN AN aMMMazing presentation is where we need to ensure that our presentation *motivates* our audience to do the goal that you identified for them.

If you have gone through the process of selecting only the most meaningful information to accomplish your goal and have been able to apply the rule of three to make it memorable, then your presentation will be inherently motivational for your audience. But there are some additional steps you can take to further encourage your audience to act.

INCLUDE A CLEAR CALL TO ACTION

You can't expect your audience to act if you don't make it clear what they should do with the information. You need to include a clear call to action along with specific steps for your audience to take. Don't leave it up to them to figure out what they are supposed to do. Tell them exactly what you'd like them to do, and show them how to do it.

> **TIP! Give your audience a clear call to action with specific steps.**

If you have already answered the third of the three essential questions, "What do I want my audience to do?" then perhaps your call to action can be an explicit request to do it. In the example in the previous chapter where the presenter had a goal for the audience to read Stephen Covey's book, his call to action would be exactly that!

Your call to action might include a specific next step to take, where to get more information, or who to contact with questions.

However, there are a couple of pitfalls that can get in the way of truly motivating your audience with a clear call to action. This is something that all presenters must avoid: going over time and allowing questions to derail or undermine your presentation.

YOUR PRESENTATION WILL NOT BE MOTIVATIONAL IF YOU GO OVER TIME

We've all been there, sitting in a presentation where the presenter starts going over. One minute, two minutes, five minutes—oh man, you have somewhere to be! Some people start awkwardly packing their bags. A few brave souls get up and leave. There is nothing more frustrating for an audience than a presenter going over time. I know this because I've done it myself as a presenter and have read enough angry reviews of people who felt frustrated when I did, so I try to avoid it at all costs!

RESPECT THE CLOCK

TIP! Don't go over time. Ever.

It is so disappointing to put all of that effort into a presentation, to have worked hard to identify the most meaningful information, and to have whittled down tons of content into three easy-to-remember concepts, only for the audience to mainly remember that the presenter made them late for their next meeting or class.

Such social awkwardness does not exist in a virtual presentation setting; your attendees will simply drop off and join their next meeting or class on time.

> **TIP! If your time runs out before you have made it through your content, stop talking.**

After the clock runs out, chances are your audience is not going to be paying much attention to anything you say because they will be thinking about where they need to be next. If you have not accomplished the goal of your presentation within your allotted time, then nothing you say after your time is up will make any difference. You have already lost their attention. That may sound harsh, but it's true.

So how do you ensure that you cover all of your key points and finish a clear call to action, without going over time? There is literally only one way to do it: You need to talk through your presentation out loud and time yourself before you present.

There are no shortcuts to this. You cannot accurately estimate how long your presentation will be just by flipping through your slides silently in your head. We'll expand more on this in Section 3, but the inexplicable fact is this: If you commit to composing a presentation before you deliver it, you will know exactly how long it is before you present it. This is the same way a singer knows exactly how long each song of theirs is! If you don't compose a presentation and just wing it live, there's no way to ensure you will end on time.

YOUR PRESENTATION WILL NOT BE MOTIVATIONAL IF QUESTIONS DERAIL IT

Handling questions is often one of the areas of presenting that presenters are most anxious about. You can allow time for questions—but don't allow questions to make you go over time.

Here are a few tips to help you handle questions in a way that will ensure your presentation stays motivational, regardless of what questions come your way.

You may wonder why we are talking about questions at all. Surely, this aspect is related to the delivery of the presentation rather than the creation of the presentation? Not so. When you compose your presentation, you need to plan for *if, when,* and *for how long* you intend to take questions from your audience. When your audience expects to have the opportunity to ask questions, but you run out of time, this can negatively affect the impact of your whole presentation. I've read hundreds of presentation reviews stating, "The presenter didn't allow time for questions." If your scenario demands it, make sure to include a specific time period where you will take questions.

DON'T FINISH WITH QUESTIONS

What is often the last slide in a presentation deck? It's the "Questions?" slide! This is the part of the presentation where you can lose control of the room and the clock. It is a good idea to take questions at the end of your presentation, but make sure that questions are not what you end your presentation on. Three things can happen when you ask for questions at the end, and only one of them is good:

1. Hands shoot up and people ask you positive questions, such as "Where do I sign?" or "When can we get started?" or "Why was this presentation so good?!"

2. There is an awkward silence. The problem with silence, when no one asks a question, is that it's wide open to interpretation. Either you have blown people's minds and completely satisfied every thought and whim in their minds, or they just want you to stop talking. There really is no way to tell for sure. At the very least, this can leave your presentation on an uncomfortable note.

3. You get negative or difficult questions. Sometimes people are genuinely upset about something, and because you have the mic, you get the brunt of it. It's brutal when this is the last thing your audience hears.

If number 1 happens, excellent—clearly your audience is motivated!

However, if number 2 or 3 happens, your well-crafted presentation can finish on a flat or sour note. If there are no questions, it's an awkward way to end. If the questions go badly, then it's a terrible way to end.

TIP! Don't end with questions. Yes, include time for questions at the end, but have a well-prepared closing statement.

Here's an awesome tip that will help you stay in control and finish strong, regardless of whether you just experienced 1, 2, or

3: *Finish with a strong, positive, well-prepared statement after the questions.* This might be your call to action, the next steps, or even a humorous quote. Just have something in mind to say to ensure that you finish strong. If there are still a lot of hands up, it's OK to tell people that you would love to take more questions but you are out of time, and you can follow up with them afterward.

REPEAT ALL QUESTIONS

While we are on the topic of questions, it's worth stating this here because you can never be reminded of it too often:

Repeat the questions, every time! There are two very good reasons for this.

1. To make sure everyone hears the question

Obviously, if there are no microphones for the audience, by repeating the question over the microphone, you are ensuring that everyone hears the question that you are about to answer. But even when people ask the question into a microphone and everyone heard it, you should still repeat it back. Why? That is the second reason.

2. To clarify that you are answering the right question

When you repeat the question back, you are allowing yourself time (even a few seconds) to formulate a response. As you repeat the question in your own words, you are confirming that you have heard what they are asking, so you can ask it back to them and say, "Is this what you mean?"

Why did I just stray into the area of presentation delivery when I stated that this book was focused on writing presentations? Basically, it's all about how you plan out your time as you are writing. Repeating back the questions takes time that you should allow for as you prepare the content and time yourself.

You should never go into a presentation scared of difficult questions. While you are preparing, you should be anticipating difficult questions and trying to include the answers (or at least address these topics) proactively in your presentation. If you expect questions that simply don't have a good answer, at least make sure you have a strategy in mind for how to handle them—the best defense is offense.

And finally, don't be afraid to end early. If there are no more questions and you still have a few minutes left, say your closing statement and give everyone some extra time back in their day—they'll appreciate it.

SUMMARY OF
THE AMMMAZING
PRESENTATION THEORY

AN AMMMAZING PRESENTATION IS—

- *Meaningful* to your target audience
- *Memorable* because you have incorporated memory aid techniques
- *Motivational* because you have set forth a clear goal for your audience, have respected their time, and have ended on a positive note

Knowing what to do in a presentation is one thing, but knowing how to put this theory into practice is quite another. In the next section, we will discuss the structure of a presentation and will provide a blueprint you can use for all of your presentations. Then, in Section 3, we'll provide a step-by-step method for writing your presentations that incorporates everything discussed so far.

How to Ensure Your Presentation Is aMMMazing

Meaningful

1. Answer the three essential questions before you start creating content.

2. Tailor *every* presentation to the audience.

3. Make your presentation for your audience, not for yourself.

Memorable

1. Use the rule of three.

2. Find a hook such as an analogy, story, quote, statistic, etc.

3. Use mnemonics and repetition.

Motivational

1. Include a clear call to action.

2. Allow time for questions—within your available time!

3. End with a strong closing statement.

SECTION 2:
SECRETS OF
STRUCTURE

—

A REPEATABLE STRUCTURE YOU CAN USE FOR ALL OF YOUR PRESENTATIONS

INTRODUCTION TO THE
SECRETS OF STRUCTURE

THE CONCEPT OF STRUCTURE IS one of the most fundamental, and often most overlooked, elements of presentations. To
understand the value of having a clear structure in your presentations, let's go back to our songwriting analogy.

There's a repeatable structure within songs that has been in use
from the Beatles to U2 to Ed Sheeran. Radio-friendly pop and
rock songs have a clear structure. Here's a common song structure:

Others have a similar structure, like this:

When you listen to pop songs on the radio, almost all of them
are structured like that. Now you may have a popular song in mind

that has a different structure altogether, and that's fine, but it still has a structure, which is our point!

Did you also notice how the classic song structure applies the rule of three? A song has three distinct parts: verse, bridge, and chorus.

Or you could group the song into the three parts like this:

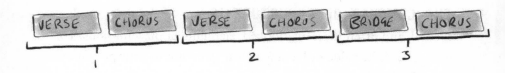

Similarly, presentations that are easy on the ear also have a clear structure. This general concept seems obvious, but it's not! Many presentations that you hear have a one-part structure like this:

Starting to talk does not necessarily count as an "introduction," and stopping talking does not mean that you have "concluded" your presentation. The words "so that's all I have to say" often seem to come out of nowhere and bring the presentation to a screeching halt rather than a satisfying end.

Every presentation should have the following basic structure:

Each part should be distinct. Each part should be well prepared. Each part should have a clear purpose.

The audience should clearly know when the introduction is over and when the main body of the presentation has begun. Similarly, the audience should also recognize when you've covered all of the main content and are bringing the presentation to a conclusion.

In Section 1, we described how your overall presentation should be meaningful, memorable, and motivational. To help us understand the true purpose of the distinct parts of your presentation, we can also assign one of the *M*'s to each of these sections to help identify the primary goal of each part.

You should strive to write a *meaningful introduction*, a *memorable body*, and a *motivational conclusion*.

- The purpose of the introduction is to establish why the information is meaningful to your audience.

- The purpose of the main body is to cover your key ideas in a memorable way.

- The purpose of the conclusion is to motivate your audience to take action.

Let's reveal the secrets of how to make each part of your presentation aMMMazing. In this section, we'll talk about the structure of your slide deck to give you a framework on which to build when we discuss the writing process in Section 3.

Story Time!

I attended a presentation where the presenter began by announcing, "I'm delighted to say, I will not be using PowerPoint!" That was met with rapturous applause from the audience. I shifted in my seat, genuinely thinking to myself, "This is going to be good!" Except it wasn't. You see, for the next forty-five minutes the presenter droned on and on, telling anecdote after anecdote . . .

There was absolutely no structure to his presentation whatsoever. He didn't have an introduction beyond that statement, he didn't stress any key points or ideas, and he didn't have a conclusion. He just blabbed until he stopped blabbing. The overall impression that the presenter gave (to me at least) was that he hadn't prepared anything; he just showed up and started talking. In a weird turn of events, on this specific occasion, the lack of slides made the whole thing even more uncomfortable because there was nowhere else to look, and as I was sitting right up front in the room, I felt trapped! It was the rarest of rare occasions where I would have enjoyed some wordy slides to read.

I'll talk more about slides later, but for now, the point is this: Not using slides is commendable if you don't need them. In fact, while visuals can enhance your presentation and help you support your key ideas, your presentation can still have all the hallmarks of being aMMMazing without any visuals at all. Not preparing anything, having no structure or key points, and just getting up to talk and making up your content on the spot for the allotted time is not commendable. In fact, it's a waste of everyone's time.

So, if you decide to go bold and present with no slides, that's excellent—but make sure you deliver an aMMMazing presentation with a clear structure.

What about presentations that are "panel discussions," "interviews," or "conversations"? Some presentations call for multiple people to participate in a conversational style of delivery, with perhaps one person interviewing another, two people going back and forth in a conversation, or one person moderating a panel of several people. This style of delivery can be engaging, but equally, if it's not well thought out, it can be immensely boring and dull. When a conversation between multiple people meanders all over the place, it can be difficult for the audience to follow or identify the most important points being discussed.

If you are responsible for running a session like this, there's an easy principle to keep in mind: Structure the conversation the same way as you would a regular presentation.

There seems to be a belief out there that the more people that are involved in a presentation, the less preparation is required ahead of time. Some people reason that a few prep calls are all it takes to be ready to take the stage.

I have found that having multiple people involved in the delivery of information often requires *more* work and preparation to ensure that the content and conversation is structured in a way that makes it meaningful, memorable, and motivational to the audience.

Going back to our song analogy, with live performances of a song there are three main phases involved:

1. Writing

2. Rehearsing

3. Performing

Then think about who is involved in each phase:

1. Writing—the songwriters

2. Rehearsing—the performers

3. Performing—the performers

Applying these same phases to presentations, those involved in panel discussions or interview-style sessions (the performers) skip the first and second phases of the writing process and go straight to the performance. No wonder sessions like that can be hit or miss!

If you are the writer of the session, then you should apply all of the concepts covered in this book. Once you've structured the conversation in a way that establishes why the information is important to the audience, flows well, highlights some key ideas, and finishes strong, then you should assemble your other performers to rehearse well enough for a flawless performance.

What kind of presenter are you, jazz or pop?

While we are talking about structure within our presentations, you might be realizing that this results in a specific presentation style, and you may be wondering if this will fit *your* style.

Let's bring this into the context of our music analogy. You may be a fan of jazz and ready to argue the point that some of the best jazz music has been the result of live, impromptu fiddlings and isn't structured but "just flows, man!" (in a beatnik-type manner).

I'll not argue with you there (especially because I have Miles Davis playing in the background as I write this), but I will say that in those cases the music has been created by experts—true artistes of their instruments who have played for years and have practiced their craft with other like-minded virtuosos in a variety of settings. Hats off to the people (musicians and presenters) who have honed their skills so well that they can ultimately get on any stage, in any setting, and create brilliance on the fly! It also must be said that these people live and breathe their craft and are constantly honing their discipline.

If you define your presentation style as a "jazz singer" and like to get up on stage and "see what happens," while resisting the idea of composing structured presentations, I tip my hat to you. You have to be really good at your craft to pull that off, and I have seen it done well on occasion.

However, not to enrage any jazz lovers out there, but jazz is not the most popular musical style (in fact, it's the least popular, according to a study I found after a quick Google search). Jazz is one of the most difficult musical styles to master. Some forms of jazz are certainly an acquired taste. For the uninitiated, jazz can be difficult to follow.

Similarly, it can be hard to tune in to a presenter who is making up the message on the fly. As a presenter wanders from one topic to the next, it's easy for your mind to wander, and usually in a different direction.

As you think about honing your presentation style, if you can truly commit to your craft as a "jazz" type of presenter, where you riff on and vocalize whatever springs to mind in front of an audience, by all means, go for it!

If you want to ensure that you will deliver something worth listening to every time, however, think about developing your style as a "pop" presenter and performing well-structured, radio-friendly presentations you've already composed.

Why? Pop songs are easy on the ear. They move the listener by tuning into popular ideas that are meaningful, like relationships, good times, and dancing. They are memorable and get stuck in your head. They are motivational because it makes you do things without even realizing it, like tap your foot. It's hard to tap your foot to obscure and complicated jazz, am I right? All those polyrhythms disrupt your foot-tapping!

continued

It takes years of study to earn respect as a jazz musician, but with the right tools in hand, anyone can write and record a catchy pop song. Radio-friendly pop songs follow a formula and a clear, repeatable structure, and so do aMMMazing presentations. In Section 3, I will show you how to write catchy presentations. And maybe one day, I'll write a book on some of the highly obscure, weird, and wonderful presentation techniques out there, and liken them to acid jazz, but that will have to wait for another day. With that out of the way, let's examine the structure of an aMMMazing presentation!

4

A MEANINGFUL INTRODUCTION

THE PURPOSE OF THE INTRODUCTION is to establish why the topic is meaningful to your audience and set up the rest of your presentation.

Your introduction is your opportunity to grab your listeners' attention and make them care about the information you are about to deliver. How long do you have to do this? Well, a quick Google search will provide you with a range of answers, from 2.7 seconds to 15 seconds. Without getting into the supporting hypotheses and well-researched data around each number, the point is that you have seconds to grab the attention of your audience, not minutes. You have to say enough in the opening seconds of your presentation to grab their attention and make them want to listen to everything else you are going to say.

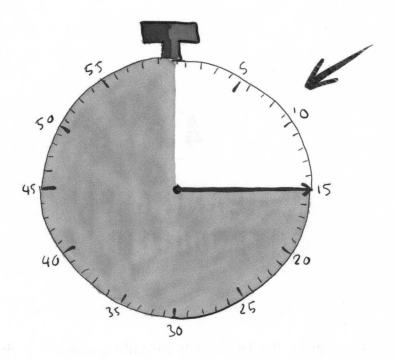

What do you generally say in the first 15 seconds of your presentation? Are you wasting those valuable seconds on unnecessary introductions? Do you just start talking and see what comes out? Or are your opening words always deliberate, carefully chosen, and well rehearsed?

In a meaningful introduction, you should grab the attention of your audience with your opening words, establish why the information is important to them, and then set up the rest of your presentation for success. Let's examine each of these one by one.

GRAB THE AUDIENCE'S ATTENTION WITH YOUR OPENING WORDS

Choose your opening words carefully and practice exactly how you will say them. Personally, I like to open with an attention-grabbing or surprising statement, such as my hook. This might be a detail from an analogy I'm about to expand on, a quote, a statistic, a news item, a story, an example, or a question—something unexpected that will encourage the audience to pay attention.

Sometimes, I like to have the audience wonder, *Where is he going with this?* after my opening statement. And then I enjoy saying, "So you might be wondering what on earth that has to do with [my topic]?" and proceed to spell out the relationship. When done right, this can be an engaging way to introduce the detail you are about to cover.

If you try this tactic though, be careful. You don't want to leave your audience wondering why you are discussing something seemingly irrelevant to them for too long, so make sure you get to the point quickly. Challenge yourself to open with a surprising statement rather than a predictable self-introduction—it can be fun, and it definitely grabs your listeners' attention.

ESTABLISH WHY THE INFORMATION IS IMPORTANT

If you have not yet read the book *Start with Why* by Simon Sinek, put that on your list because it's an excellent read. He clearly proves that first establishing why a topic is important to the listener, before getting into the *what*, makes all communications exponentially more engaging and meaningful. There are some very powerful examples in his book demonstrating that arranging your content to start with the *why* of the topic can turn simple information into spectacular inspiration.

The standout example he uses is the ad that famed explorer Sir Ernest Shackleton reportedly placed in a newspaper when looking for people to join his mission to sail across Antarctica in 1914:[3]

MEN WANTED FOR HAZARDOUS JOURNEY. SMALL WAGES, BITTER COLD, LONG MONTHS OF COMPLETE DARKNESS, CONSTANT DANGER, SAFE RETURN DOUBTFUL. HONOUR AND RECOGNITION IN CASE OF SUCCESS. —SIR ERNEST SHACKLETON

This ad accomplished its goal because Shackleton found a crew, but it did more than that. That boat ultimately got stuck in ice and stranded for almost two years, yet not a single life was lost. Sinek reasons that the sense of purpose these men signed up for was so strong that it helped these men endure the very hazards they were warned about.

An ad in a newspaper, like an introduction to a presentation, has a few seconds to capture someone's attention and their imagination. I like to imagine that if Shackleton were delivering a presentation with the goal of convincing people to go on this journey with him, that he would have opened his speech with these very words. Establishing why your topic is important is an excellent way to use your opening seconds.

Besides being a tactic to grab your audience's attention, a carefully chosen analogy, story, quote, example, statistic, question, or news item can also help you to establish why the information matters. Beginning with why can help you establish an emotional

---

3   Simon Sinek, *Start with Why: How Great Leaders Inspire Everyone to Take Action* (New York: Penguin Group, 2009).

connection to the relevancy of your topic before you get into the detail, and help your audience want to stick with you to the end.

Let's put the idea of opening with a powerful or surprising statement and the concept of "start with why" together and think of them in the context of most slide-driven presentations. These are typically the first two slides of a presentation:

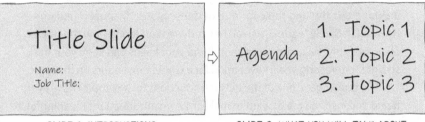

SLIDE 1: INTRODUCTIONS   SLIDE 2: WHAT YOU WILL TALK ABOUT

Here's the problem with that: When the first valuable, attention-grabbing seconds of your presentation are taken up with you introducing yourself and covering what you are going to talk about, your audience may not yet understand why they should care about any of it and begin tuning you out immediately. This is starting with *what* rather than *why*.

When structuring your slides, commit to having at least one slide in between the title slide and the agenda slide.

WHO YOU ARE (IF NECESSARY)   WHY YOUR INFORMATION IS IMPORTANT   WHAT YOU WILL TALK ABOUT

This simple trick will force you to think through what you need to say to establish why your content is important to your listener, and include that in your presentation.

Story Time!

I once attended a health and safety "train the trainer" seminar, which included this thrilling topic for one of the sessions: "Manual Handling—How to Lift Safely." I admit to walking in there wondering how the trainer could possibly make the concept of "bend your knees and keep your back straight" interesting at all, never mind for a whole three hours on the topic.

The trainer gave one of the best introductions for any topic I have ever heard and inspired me to want to make my own introductions meaningful to my audience.

You see, he didn't start talking about boxes or rules or giving any instructions. He started by showing an image of something I didn't expect at all: the human spine.

He then went on to describe the relationship between the vertebrae, discs, and nervous system. He described a spinal disc as a jelly donut (I've never looked at one the same) and actually squashed one to show the jelly coming out! He went on to describe (in graphic detail) the condition of sciatica and what happens when a disc ruptures and touches the spinal column, and then he shared a couple of distressing real-world examples. He flowed from that topic into the principles of weights and levers, showing that weight applied to one side of an evenly balanced lever requires an equal amount of pressure on the other side to keep it level. Then, he showed how this math changed when the central point moved away from the center of the lever and how this significantly multiplied the pressure needed to keep the lever in balance.

He went on to connect the dots by showing us how the spine is like an off-center lever on the lumbar region of your back, and then showed the mathematical equation proving that incorrectly lifting something weighing only twenty pounds could exert more than six hundred pounds of pressure on your spine and cause horrendous injuries.

By the time he actually got to the instructions of how to lift correctly, we were all hanging on his every word. I've never been so nervous to lift an empty box in my life! It was years ago, and I still remember it very well, so he did something right!

After you have opened with a powerful statement and established why your audience should care about what you are about to say, you should then include a preview of what you will cover.

Make sure your introduction includes some *why* statements and ideas: why your audience should care about the topic, why they should listen to the end, why they should ultimately take action. A wise presenter includes whys in their introduction.

SET UP THE REST OF THE PRESENTATION FOR SUCCESS

Toward the end of your introduction, but before you get into your main content, you should preview your agenda. Here you can point out your three main ideas or topics you've worked so hard to arrange your material around. This is the "tell them what you are going to tell them" part of the famous phrase.

Be careful with the overall length of your introduction too. If you refer to our structure diagram on page 67, you'll see that the introduction is proportionally shorter than the body of the presentation. If you end up with too much content in your intro and find that your introduction is the longest part of the whole presentation, you probably need to restructure it.

BUT WHAT ABOUT SPEAKER INTRODUCTIONS?

Short answer: It depends. The title slide probably already has your name and title on it, which may be as much information as your audience really needs to know. Or, if someone is going to introduce you, let them share something relevant about you and your experience so that you can begin with a powerful opening line. Your presence as the speaker often comes with implied credibility. If you try too hard to establish your credibility, it can have the opposite effect.

This is where the "depends" part comes in, however. If there's something specific about your experience that is relevant to your topic and goal, that can itself serve as a highly attention-grabbing introduction. For example, I once heard retired US Navy Vice Admiral Bill Sullivan speak on the topic of leadership. He introduced himself by discussing the ships he'd captained, along with some of the potentially world-changing circumstances he'd navigated. Powerful? Yes. Relevant? Absolutely! He had the audience eating out of the palm of his hand as he continued!

If no one has introduced you and you feel that you need to introduce yourself, keep your introduction brief. Remember, the presentation is about your audience, not about you, and you have mere seconds to grab their attention.

How to Make Your Introduction Meaningful

1. Capture your audience's attention immediately.

- Ensure your opening words are purposefully chosen and well prepared.

- Include statements that are attention-grabbing, perhaps surprising.

- Do not begin with the agenda or lengthy, unnecessary speaker introductions.

2. Create an emotional connection.

- Establish why the information is relevant to your target audience.

- Reinforce relevancy with an analogy, a story, a quote, an example, questions, statistics, or a news item.

- Ensure the introduction supports your goal for the audience (explicitly or implicitly).

3. Set up the rest of the presentation for success.

- Preview your three main ideas or topics to be covered (the agenda).

- Ensure your introduction is an appropriate length for your overall presentation.

- Compel your audience to listen to what you have to say.

5

A MEMORABLE BODY

THE PURPOSE OF THE PRESENTATION body is to present your content in a memorable way.

This is the part where you get into the main content of your material—the middle "tell them" in the "tell them, tell them, tell them" principle.

So far, we have established that your overall presentation should have three main sections: the introduction, the body, and your conclusion. The body of your presentation is where you will cover the most information and should be arranged around three main topics, should be easy to follow, and should include just the *right* amount of information. Let's discuss each of these.

USE THE RULE OF THREE

As we discussed in Chapter 2, the rule of three is a very powerful memory aid. Beyond catchy three-part phrases, you should use the rule of three to organize the information within the body of your presentation around your three ideas or topics.

When you do that, it inherently facilitates the memory-aiding technique of repetition. As we just covered, you can preview your three main points in your introduction, and then during the body, you can cover each point sequentially.

When structuring my slide decks, I like to use my agenda slide as a "transition" slide between each of my three main sections. I highlight or bold the section I'm about to get in to on the slide, then revisit it as I transition between sections:

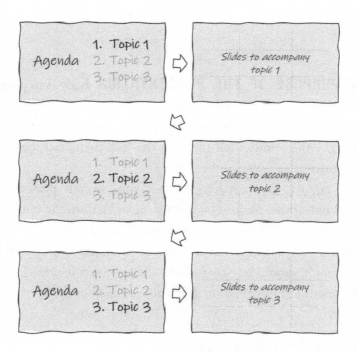

These types of transition slides help you to make it clear that you are moving from one thought or section to the next.

The slide format depicted here is just for illustrative purposes.

I don't often actually have the word *agenda* on my slides. I'll often replace that with my main theme or topic, or simply list the three points I'm going to cover, perhaps over a full-screen image relating to the subject at hand.

Transition slides make it easy for your audience to know where they are within the context of your overall presentation, and help them understand that you are making progress through your intended points.

> **I sometimes call transition slides "palate cleansers," like a refreshing sorbet a server at a fancy restaurant gives you between courses to make the next dish that is presented as tasty as possible.**

When you repeatedly show your agenda again and again like this, it allows you to pause, to summarize your key idea from the section you just covered, and then to transition to your next key idea.

The true beauty of applying the three-point-agenda rule is that this same structure applies whether you are talking for five minutes or sixty minutes. Your three points are the same, but the amount of supporting detail changes according to the time you have available.

While an accordion may not be the most fashionable of musical instruments, it is one I am quite fond of, and I like to compare the concept of the three-point agenda to one.

5 MINUTE VERSION   ONE HOUR VERSION

If you have a short presentation, you will present your three main points with just the essential supporting details. If you have a longer presentation, you will still present the same three main points, but you will include more details, examples, and information.

Like squeezing and expanding an accordion according to the length of the note you want to play, you can shrink or expand the detail supporting your three main points depending on the length of your presentation. It's the same note, just with more air. Or, in your presentation, it's the same idea, but just with more talking in support of it.

A word of caution on the three-point-agenda rule: It's not a matter of just creating a simple-looking agenda and then proceeding to cover your information as a stream of consciousness until you end. To do this effectively requires you to actually arrange your material into three well-balanced sections that are easy to follow.

EASY TO FOLLOW

You want to make sure that your information is presented in a logical and understandable manner. As you transition between your key points and sections, give careful attention to your phrasing. Sometimes you need to use very specific language to help your audience follow where you are going.

It's a good idea to carefully word "linking" statements as you transition between each of your three key ideas. Here's an example: "So now that we've established the first point, you may be wondering [insert thought]. This takes us nicely into our next section . . ." This is a classic (and generic) example of a transition statement to help your audience make the leap from one point to the next.

As you develop your content, make sure that any analogies, stories, quotes, and statistics that you include are relevant and relatable to the audience and support the key point being made or the overall goal of the presentation. If you are going to use analogies, use them carefully and deliberately. Analogies can be a fantastic way to drive home a complex topic or idea, but don't make them up as you go. I've witnessed speakers run into trouble by coming up with analogies on the spot that inadvertently allude to ideas that they did not intend to include. The safest course of action is this: Avoid making up any new content on the fly during a presentation. Analogies and similar content are great to use as a tactic, but do so when you write your presentation!

INCLUDE JUST THE RIGHT AMOUNT OF INFORMATION

The main body of the presentation should move along at a steady pace, without feeling as though it's dragging or going too fast.

A symptom of including too much information is if you find yourself rushing or "skipping slides" to get through it. Generally, you only realize this when you are delivering the presentation, and by then it's too late. We'll talk more about the role that visuals should play later, but it's worth stating here that your slides should complement what you are saying, not drive what you are saying. Do you find yourself beholden to your slides and unable to go faster or slower, because you get drawn into a vortex where you feel the need to explain every detail on every slide as the clock marches beyond your allotted time? That's a clear sign that you've included *way* too much material. It's also a clear sign that you have skipped over several essential steps in the writing process, which we'll get into in Section 3.

Have you ever seen one of those dolls where you pull the string and it talks? When the string runs out, the doll stops talking. Then, when you pull the string, it talks again. Some presenters are like that doll. They click their slide and talk until they run out of things to say, then click the next slide, and it happens all over again.

If you have prepared an aMMMazing presentation, you will not be like a string doll.

How to Make Your Body Memorable

1. Use the rule of three.

- Ensure the body comes between a distinct introduction and a clear conclusion.

- Arrange the information in the body around three easy-to-remember ideas.

- Use repetition (and mnemonics) to reinforce your key ideas.

2. Be easy to follow.

- Present your information in a logical and understandable manner.

- Include "linking" statements to clearly transition between sections and ideas.

- Ensure analogies, stories, quotes, statistics, and so on are well thought out, relevant, and relatable.

3. Include just the right amount of information.

- If you are using visuals, ensure they appropriately support the words being spoken.

- Make your three main points clear, and fill your time with the appropriate amount of supporting detail.

- Allocate an appropriate amount of time for the information without rushing or skipping slides.

6

A MOTIVATIONAL
CONCLUSION

A CONCLUSION SHOULD SUMMARIZE AND reinforce your key ideas and give your audience clear steps to take next.

The conclusion is one area that many speakers pay the least attention to. I observe a lot of speakers open strong—perhaps with an excellent analogy, quote, or other attention-grabbing technique—and cover their material well, but then end their presentation abruptly or awkwardly, or they run out of time. Your conclusion is your opportunity to motivate your audience to take action.

Have you ever heard the expression "The last thing you say is the first thing they remember"? Give some thought to that as it relates to your conclusion.

The conclusion is the part of your presentation that can truly make your key points memorable, address any questions your audience has, and include a specific call to action or next steps. Let's examine each of these.

SUMMARY OF YOUR MAIN POINTS

This is the "tell them what you told them" part. I like to do this by revisiting my agenda slide and perhaps adding the word "summary" to it, then use it to briefly summarize my key points.

Here's an amazing trick: Revisit a concept from your introduction in your conclusion. Did you open with a quote, analogy, story, or other hook? If you did, mention that same concept again in your conclusion to tie a nice bow on the end of the presentation. Perhaps you can restate a phrase or idea from your introduction that now has a lot more meaning, given the context of your presentation. Sometimes, if I start with a famous quote in my introduction, I'll restate that quote and look for another quote from the same person or another famous quote on the same topic to end on a satisfying note. If I started with an analogy in my introduction, I'll mention another detail related to the analogy in the conclusion to drive the key points home. It is very gratifying for you and your audience when you bring your presentation full circle.

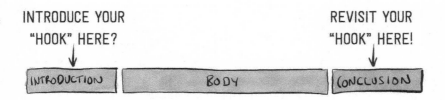

MANAGE QUESTIONS

These are typically the last two slides in a deck:

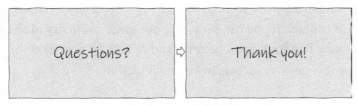

TYPICAL ENDING TO A PRESENTATION

As we discussed in Chapter 3, *prepare a strong concluding statement to say once questions are over.*

You should include time for questions at the end of your presentation, but don't end on them. Ending on questions can end your presentation on a flat note. You need to manage questions well to ensure that they do not derail the goal of your presentation or make you go over time.

To avoid this pitfall, make sure that you always include at least one slide after the "Questions?" slide and before your "Thank you!" slide. This trick will remind you to always prepare a strong closing statement.

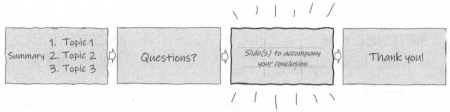

1. Topic 1
Summary 2. Topic 2 ⇨   Questions?   ⇨   *Slide(s) to accompany your conclusion*   ⇨   Thank you!
3. Topic 3

A MUCH BETTER ENDING TO A PRESENTATION

CALL TO ACTION

As you conclude your presentation, make sure you also include a clear call to action for the audience. Outline the next steps for your audience: what to do, where to get more information, and who to contact. If you can provide a one-page summary of the key ideas as a handout, even better—and it will be easy to do if you follow the steps to success in our final section.

Land the Plane!

Your presentation can be likened to an airplane you are piloting, with your audience as your passengers. An airplane flight has three main parts: the takeoff, the flight path, and the landing.

Which parts of the flight demand the most attention from the pilot? Generally, the takeoff and landing. The pilot handles takeoff manually and then utilizes the autopilot once in the air. Then, when it comes to landing, the pilot must be fully engaged once again.

So how does this relate to a presentation? As a presenter, you are the pilot of a three-part journey.

Your introduction is like the takeoff, where you float new ideas and (hopefully) compel the audience enough to stay with you on the journey. Carefully crafted, specific wording is key.

The body is the part where the plane is in the air and you are covering the most ground in your presentation. I'm certainly not saying that you should go on autopilot and fall asleep at the wheel! But the body of the presentation is the part where you can get into a comfortable rhythm talking through your material.

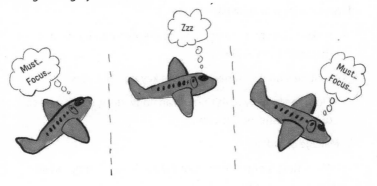

The conclusion is where you need to land the plane. Just like an actual flight, you need to prepare your "passengers" for landing and successfully bring all of your thoughts and ideas to a satisfying conclusion. Again, carefully prepared words and statements are the key to bringing your ideas home.

Many presentations leave the listeners hanging in midair, with no summary, conclusion, or resolution. Don't do that! Make sure you land the plane in your conclusion.

Pay the most attention to your takeoff and your landing—your introduction and your conclusion. Even if you are an experienced presenter and you can kind of go on autopilot in the main body of your presentation, with an extemporaneous delivery style, you should still give careful and deliberate attention to your word choice and phrasing as you introduce your presentation, as you transition between key ideas, and as you conclude your talk. If you don't have time to run through the entire presentation out loud before you present, at least rehearse your introduction and conclusion so you can ensure a smooth takeoff and landing for your audience.

One final thought! Just because an experienced pilot successfully executed a takeoff and landing on their last flight, do you think they will pay any less attention to their next flight? No way! Every single flight demands as much attention as the last, much like your presentations.

How to Make Your Conclusion Motivational

1. Summarize your main points.

- Make it clear that the body of the presentation is over and the conclusion has begun.

- Include a brief summary of all the key points discussed.

- Close the loop by revisiting the analogy, story, quote, and so on used in the introduction.

2. Manage questions.

- Allow time for questions from the audience (if appropriate).

- Anticipate difficult questions and have a strategy to handle them.

- Prepare a strong closing statement to share after questions have concluded.

3. Include a call to action.

- Specify a clear call to action for the audience.

- Outline next steps, what to do, who to contact, and where to get more information.

- Provide a one-page summary of the key ideas as a handout, rather than the entire slide deck.

SUMMARY OF SECRETS OF STRUCTURE

IN THIS SECTION, WE DISCUSSED how to structure your information into an introduction, a three-part body, and a conclusion.

In the Appendix, you will find the Slide Deck Structure Template, which consolidates all of the key ideas covered in this section. The template provides a starting framework on which you can build the rest of the visuals to support each section and key ideas.

It's worth repeating that showing the agenda slide multiple times is not redundant because it helps your audience to clearly see, understand, and follow the structure of your information throughout. This simple technique can be one of the best ways to make your presentation aMMMazing.

When you apply the concepts in this section, it means that your presentation will have a minimum of thirteen slides before you begin (Refer to the Slide Deck Structure Template on page 197):

1. The title slide

2. The introduction slide

3. The agenda slide showing all three key ideas

4. The agenda slide with your *first* key idea highlighted

5. At least one slide to support your first key idea

6. The agenda slide with your *second* key idea highlighted

7. At least one slide to support your second key idea

8. The agenda slide with your *third* key idea highlighted

9. At least one slide to support your third key idea

10. The agenda slide again as a summary of all three key ideas

11. Your "questions" slide

12. The slide to support your strong concluding statement

13. Your "thank you" slide

What I love about using this format to build my own presentations is that it inherently includes the three *M*'s without having to think too hard about them:

- **Meaningful**—Includes an introduction slide between the title slide and the agenda, where you should establish why the information is important prior to what you will talk about.

- **Memorable**—Utilizes the following concepts:
  - Rule of three, with three main parts and three agenda points in the body
  - Repetition by using the agenda slide as a preview of the

key ideas at the beginning, to remind the audience of the key points throughout the body, and as a summary in the conclusion to reinforce them.

- **Motivational**—Includes a concluding slide for a strong closing statement after you have summarized and handled questions.

This format is an awesome starting place because you have already created your structure and you can then simply fill in the graphics and images for your sections. But yet, this leads to some questions.

WHAT IF MY PRESENTATION IS ONLY A FEW MINUTES LONG?

If you only have a few minutes to speak, you will need to flex this concept; otherwise the only words you'd be able to get out would be to tell them your agenda, tell them the agenda again, and then summarize the agenda—all without actually covering any detail, which would be ridiculous.

In those cases, you should still structure your presentation with an introduction, body, and conclusion, but go lighter on the number of slides you'd use to introduce, repeat, and summarize your key ideas.

WON'T THIS RESULT IN TOO MANY SLIDES?

People often ask me whether there is a maximum or ideal number of slides you should use. No. There. Is. Not.

I like to think of myself as a peaceful person. However, when someone tries to enforce a maximum number of slides I can use in a presentation, it really grinds my gears.

To be fair, I understand why someone would suggest that. We've all been bludgeoned by bullet points often enough to feel some form of enmity toward terrible slide decks. Usually, the person stipulating a maximum number of slides is trying to ensure that the attendees are not going to experience "death by PowerPoint," where presenters mindlessly read from text-heavy slides. I get it. I totally do.

However, stipulating a maximum number of slides doesn't magically turn a poor presentation into an aMMMazing one. What happens is that the presenters use a smaller font and cram even more text onto fewer slides, and the result is worse!

The reason that stipulating a maximum number of slides drives me crazy is that good slide decks are composed of imagery, visuals, or carefully selected statements to support the words. The actual slide count doesn't matter if the deck effectively supports what's being said.

For example, I will often create multiple versions of the same slides that build on each other, to make them easier to create or animate. In those situations, the audience will see one slide that looks as if it's animated, but it is made up of multiple slides in my deck. It's nonsense to try to re-create that into fewer slides to meet an arbitrary rule.

As we discussed, repeating the agenda slide can be a very effective way to help your audience follow you as you transition between sections and ideas. These palate-cleanser slides are usually up for just a few seconds and can actually help you cut down the number of words you say as you transition between sections or ideas, because your audience can clearly see you are moving on to the next section.

I have not come across a numeric formula that will stipulate the ideal number of slides for an effective presentation. That's like saying there's a maximum number of instruments that should be in a song. Sometimes the most beautiful songs use one or two instruments only, while others are recorded with an entire orchestra and choir. If all the instruments are in tune and harmonize with one another, it's magic. If they are all out of tune or all playing different songs, it's a hot mess.

It's not the number of instruments that matters. What matters is the quality of the song.

Similarly, it's not the number of slides that matters. What matters is the quality of the presentation. An aMMMazing presentation may have no visuals, just a few, or a plethora of visual delights.

If you are planning an event and want the presenters to use slideware correctly—and not deliver death by bullet point—rather than stipulate a maximum number of slides, perhaps encourage them to apply the principles in this book well in advance of their presentations!

SECTION 3:
THE JAM SESSION
WRITING PROCESS
—

THE GUIDE TO WRITING AN
AMMMAZING PRESENTATION

INTRODUCTION TO THE JAM SESSION WRITING PROCESS

NOW THAT WE'VE EXPLORED THE elements and structure of aMMMazing presentations, it's time to start putting these concepts together.

In Chapter 1, I asked you to choose a response to this question: **When I start working on a new presentation, the first thing I am most likely to do is**

   a. Open a slideware application and start typing.

   b. Grab a pen and paper.

   c. Ask questions.

Hopefully by now you can see the value of answer *C.* Let's spend some time expanding why this is the best answer.

This is often the writing process that many presenters use:

Step 1: Open slideware application and create a deck (in silence)

Step 2: Click through the deck, thinking of what to say (in silence)

Step 3: Talk out loud for the first time in front of the audience

Why is this not the best way to write a presentation?

When you launch a slideware application and attempt to create your entire presentation from beginning to end, there's far too much going on in your mind to think clearly.

At a bare minimum, you are thinking about what to say, what order to say it in, what your slides should look like, what imagery and colors you want to use, what existing slides you might repurpose, how much time you are trying to fill—all at once!

It can start to feel overwhelming, especially when you add in the additional questions of "who's your audience? What do they care about? What do you want them to do?" I'm sure there should be a medical code for "slide sickness," where you've spent so long shuffling slides around that you feel nauseous and need to go for a long walk to clear your head.

When presenters are thinking of what words to say at the same time as they are making slides, it's no wonder that their slide decks end up being full of words. With that writing process, the slides and the words become one and the same.

Let's go back to our songwriting analogy to illustrate the point. Creating your slides while writing your presentation would be like a musician creating the stage lighting and music video backdrop for their live performance at the same time as trying to write the song!

Before you think about adding beautiful scenes, fast cars, pyrotechnics, or sweet animations to your presentation, you must write something worth listening to first. In other words, you need to compose a radio-friendly song before you create the music video.

Even if you have never written a song, it's not hard to imagine that a songwriter would play their ideas out loud as part of the writing process. A songwriter plays with their ideas to hear what sounds good and what doesn't, and then refines those ideas until they are happy with how the song sounds.

Imagine a songwriter following the same process to write a song that many people use to write presentations:

Step 1: Write the melody and lyrics for a new song on paper (in silence).

Step 2: Read through the music score several times, imagining how it sounds (in silence).

Step 3: Perform the song out loud for the first time in front of an audience.

It is hard to imagine a songwriter feeling truly confident playing a new song if they haven't even heard it themselves first, because they wouldn't have been able to ditch the things that didn't sound good to their own ears.

The "create slides and click through them in silence" approach to presentation writing is often the cause of boring and dull presentations because this method often results in slide decks with far too many words that the presenter then must "karaoke" their way through. It also creates additional anxiety for the presenter, because the presenter can only hope that the presentation will sound good, that their words will come out right, and that they will finish within the appropriate time.

To improve your presentations, you need to change your approach to writing them. Many experienced presenters will agree that you should speak out loud while you are practicing your presentations. I agree with this, but you shouldn't wait until you are practicing to hear what you are writing. If you only say your presentation out loud when you start "practicing," it can feel very frustrating going back to make changes, small or big.

And if you don't speak out loud *at all* as you write, then it can be even more frustrating to realize that you are not happy with the way your presentation sounds in front of a room full of people.

The key point here is that *speaking out loud* is an essential part of *the writing process.*

IS THERE SUCH A THING AS A PRESENTATION-WRITING *PROCESS*?

Can a creative activity, such as presentation writing, really be accomplished by following a process, though? Or should you simply make it up as you go along each time?

Well, let's think about three major ways that songs are written, and compare each of them to presentation writing.

1. A Flash of Inspiration

"Yesterday" by the Beatles, "The Cave" by Mumford & Sons, and "See You Again" by Wiz Khalifa were all reportedly written in a matter of minutes.

Remember, though, that these artists have written hundreds of songs, and these moments of inspiration that resulted in timeless classics only represent a tiny minority of their entire catalog. If an artist sat around waiting for inspiration to strike, they probably wouldn't write many songs.

Sometimes presentation ideas come to you in a flash, and the presentation almost writes itself. Before you know it, you have a presentation with a meaningful introduction, a memorable body, and a motivational conclusion, all tied together with a killer hook that is perfect for your audience. When that happens, it's amazing, but we cannot sit around waiting for inspiration to hit us every time we write presentations.

2. A Prescriptive Songwriting Process

Let's go all the way to the other end of the spectrum. Some songwriters have developed a very prescriptive process for writing, where they follow a series of steps in sequential order. These writers say that having a process to work from helps them focus, helps them make rapid progress, and provides a channel to help them organize the myriad ideas that come to their minds as they write a song.

I attended a technology conference in Nashville, Tennessee, where two highly successful songwriters delivered a keynote presentation focused on collaborative information sharing. They shared their songwriting process (which interestingly started with brainstorming ideas for lyrics before thinking about the music) and then promised to use their own process to write a song live on stage at the conference, with input from the audience of around one thousand people. They followed their step-by-step process and, in about forty-five minutes, wrote a pretty catchy song about the technology conference, live on stage. They had the whole audience singing along before they walked off. It was quite impressive!

Similarly, some experienced presenters have developed a prescriptive process for writing, in which they follow a series of steps in sequential order. Similar to experienced songwriters, these presenters often say that having a process to work from helps them focus, helps them make rapid progress, and provides a channel to help them organize the myriad ideas that come to their minds as they write their presentations.

3. A Jam Session

Now, let's examine an approach that straddles the fence between inspiration and process—writing by "jamming" ideas out loud.

Jamming is where a musician, or a number of musicians, formulates some ideas and then starts playing them out loud to find out what they sound like. As they listen to their music, the musician hears things they like and things they don't, and new ideas—possibilities for catchy riffs and lyrics—spontaneously spring to mind. Sometimes musicians will start recording to capture their ideas. This extemporaneous approach to generating songs can be highly successful. Songs such as "We Are Never Ever Getting Back Together" by Taylor Swift, the entire album *Remain in Light* by Talking Heads, and the song "Good Vibrations" by the Beach Boys were all reportedly created by artists jamming their ideas out loud and capturing them in the studio. Apparently, "Good

Vibrations" was assembled from pieces recorded in five different jam sessions from five different studios!

I was shocked when I found out that jamming is how U2 approaches their songwriting. I had assumed that they had already penned all the songs on their albums and *then* recorded them in the studio. As it turns out, their writing process involves a series of jam sessions in the studio. They fire up their instruments and start playing aloud. Ideas and concepts are thrashed out, argued over, reworked, reworked again, and then finally recorded into some of the timeless classics that we know and love today. The U2 song "Where the Streets Have No Name" almost didn't see the light of day because they couldn't get the timing in the intro right in the studio—they allegedly almost threw the whole thing out the window. But they worked it out, and the song ended up opening the *Joshua Tree* album.

Some presenters use a similar approach when writing their presentations. They speak aloud (sometimes spontaneously) to see what *sounds* good—keeping what they like and ditching what they don't—until they have created their presentation.

WHICH APPROACH IS RIGHT FOR YOU?

All of these approaches to writing presentations are valid. Since there's no way to plan for a moment of inspiration, we'll put that to the side and focus on the other two. What's the best approach then? Jamming ideas until something sounds good or following a prescriptive process?

Personally, I do both. I have a prescriptive process that I follow, and I allow myself the opportunity to jam out ideas to see what sounds good. I'm delighted to share with you the methodology that I've developed over the years while writing thousands of presentations, some for myself and many for other people—I've even picked up some awards along the way after using this method.

My methodology is called "JAM," like a jam session to write a song. JAM represents the three major phases that you go through when writing aMMMazing presentations.

JAM SESSION

Jot everything down

Articulate your words

Make your presentation tools

We will delve into each of these ideas in this section, but I'd like to draw your attention to the most significant part of this process: The words come before the visuals. As we stated at the beginning of this book, we will make visuals to match our words, not words to match our visuals. If you apply nothing else from this section, do that one thing!

When you craft the words of your presentation before you start working on any slides, you will find that your approach to slide creation will change forever (for the better!). You will realize that you do not need to be a graphic design major to create effective slide decks because your slides are not doing all the speaking—you are doing the speaking, and your slides are there to help reinforce your concepts visually. This also reduces the time you need to spend working on your slide decks because you can focus on simple visuals to support the words you will be saying.

With that in mind, I have created nine steps you can follow (three within each phase) that will help you organize your thoughts to focus on the disciplines of gathering your ideas, crafting your words, and then creating the visuals and tools to complement your presentation.

Like a jam session in songwriting, you can follow the JAM process as a general framework, or you can follow the prescriptive steps in order. Here are the three main stages, with the nine easy-to-follow steps, of the JAM process:

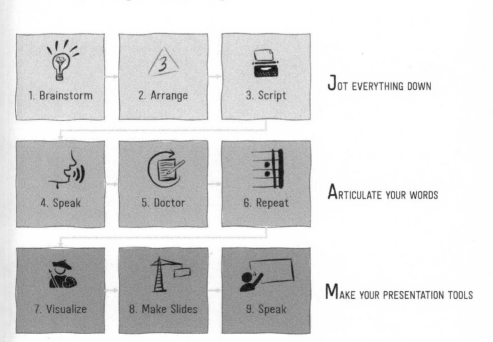

7

THE *J* IN JAM: JOT
EVERYTHING DOWN

THE FIRST PHASE OF THE JAM process involves setting aside time to gather and generate all of the content that will make up your presentation. There are a lot of methodologies and tools out there to help facilitate brainstorming and creative-thinking sessions. If you have a preferred method already, then go ahead and apply it in this phase.

Without exploring the various benefits of the concepts of "mind mapping," "thinking hats," and "lateral thinking techniques," there's one tip that works for me every single time.

To help you think creatively, use drawing tools, not typing tools.

On the surface, that might sound contradictory because we have clearly said that we will create the words first and the visuals last. I'm not talking about sketching slide ideas yet. But I am 100 percent talking about figuring out the right words to say using a pen, pencil, or marker. This is all about using tools to capture ideas as quickly as your mind thinks of them, without interrupting your thought process.

So why is using tools like a pen and paper, or a whiteboard and markers, during the brainstorming process different (or better) than firing up a slideware application and starting to type?

Think about what happens when you type in a software application. What happens when you mistype a word? The application draws your attention to it, and suddenly you are correcting spelling mistakes rather than expanding on the idea you just thought of. What happens when the line or paragraph justification is off? You immediately start fixing that. When you copy and paste from one document to another, and the new content has different formatting, you find yourself wading through font selections and paragraph settings rather than generating additional ideas. All of this interrupts your thought process and inhibits creative thinking.

I read a study about an organization that had attached brainwave sensors to two groups of people to measure their brainwave activity as they went through a brainstorming process. One group typed their ideas into a computer as they thought of them. The second group used drawing tools, such as a pen and paper, to brainstorm. The people brainstorming using drawing tools showed much greater brainwave activity in the part of the brain used for creative thinking than those using typing tools, for the reasons listed previously.

Without getting into the science and validity of the study, all I will say is this: Try it, because it is true!! It is amazing what happens when you allow your brain to think freely, and just jot down ideas as they spring to mind.

That's why I picked the word "jot" when it comes to this phase of the process. It's all to do with using the power of drawing tools, like pencils and papers or whiteboards and markers, to jot down and capture your ideas quickly, as you think of them and allowing for a free flow of thought, before you start typing your ideas up as a script.

So, how do you do it? Use the three activities under the *J* in JAM to help channel your creative thinking.

STEP 1. BRAINSTORM CONTENT IDEAS

Equipment: A room with a whiteboard, flip charts, and markers, or plenty of paper, pens, and pencils

People Involved: All subject matter experts on your topic and people who know the audience

Tools: JAM Session Writing Process Checklist (See Appendix)

In this step, we will answer the three essential questions, "empty the pantry," and explore ideas for your hook. Don't overthink, organize, or edit anything yet; just gather as much information as you can.

ANSWER THE THREE ESSENTIAL QUESTIONS

Write down the answers to the three essential questions we out-lined in Section 1. The following are some additional prompt questions to help you answer each question.

Question 1: Who is your target audience?

- Is it one or two people in the room? If so, who are they?
- Is it everyone in the room? If so, can you describe them collectively as a group?
- What other presentations will they hear at the same meeting or event, or on the same topic?

Question 2: What do they care about?

- What are the goals of the people in the room?
- What is the sentiment of your audience? Are they happy, frustrated, angry, skeptical, or neutral?
- What do they already know about this topic, and what questions do you anticipate them asking?

Question 3: What do you want them to do?

- What is the purpose of your presentation?
- What behavior, task, action, or thought process do you want them to start, stop, or change?
- What specific next steps will you ask them to take?

MINE EXISTING SOURCES—"EMPTY THE PANTRY"

While you are brainstorming, look at existing content to see if there's anything that you can incorporate. You will often discover an incredible amount of relevant information spread across existing slide decks and corporate documents, or even buried within the heads of the people in the room. However, it's easy to feel overwhelmed when there seems to be way too much information to include in your presentation. To explain how I navigate this situation, I use an analogy I call "empty the pantry."

Imagine standing in front of a totally crammed and over-full pantry, cupboard, or fridge—we've all been there. Somehow, it has become so full and cluttered that you can't find anything anymore. If you reach in for anything, there's an avalanche. How would you organize it to be able to find what you need?

It's easy: You pull everything out, lay it where you can see it (perhaps on a kitchen table), and then start to organize it.

When you do that, you start to see in one view everything that you have. Once you can see everything together, you quickly end up realizing the following:

- You have tons of duplicates—you have no recollection of buying eight cans of baked beans, but there they are!

- You have a lot of outdated stuff—you find a can of tuna that expired several years ago, and you wonder how long it's been in there.

- You don't actually have certain things that you could have sworn you had plenty of.

Large documents and slide decks with tons of information in them are very much like a cluttered pantry. There is so much information that you have no idea how to find what you need. So, how do you begin organizing the information to find what you need? You empty the pantry!

To do this, I put everything on a whiteboard or fill blank pages in a notebook. I start emptying out ideas from existing slide decks and documents and from what people add during the brainstorming session, transposing the ideas phrase by phrase onto the "table," where we can see them all together.

As you go through this exercise, you'll find that you start to naturally group like ideas together and also come to the same conclusions as you do when you are emptying an actual pantry:

- You have tons of duplicate thoughts—often you realize that the same point is being made several ways and in several places throughout the existing information. You can start to group these together.

- You have a lot of outdated stuff—there might be a favorite slide or factoid that you use all the time, but as you talk or think through it, you realize that it's old, unnecessary, or irrelevant to the goal of this presentation.

- You can't find certain content or materials that you could have sworn you had.

I encountered this exact situation several years ago in a project I worked on with a sales team. They were trying to create a presentation for prospect engagements and asked for help in combining several decks that had been created over the years by multiple people into one all-encompassing deck. As we worked through each deck, we realized that all of the decks had valuable information in them, but some had outdated content that needed to be refreshed, and some expressed similar ideas but in different ways.

The situation quickly became overwhelming because there was so much information and so many good ideas that we honestly didn't know where to start. This was the first time the "empty the pantry" analogy came to mind.

We went through each deck one by one and wrote down each unique thought or idea on a whiteboard. It was interesting to see how much content was deemed outdated or irrelevant. It was also fascinating to see how many similar thoughts were expressed in a variety of different ways, sometimes even within the same slide deck. It was obvious that we only needed to make the point once and make it strong.

During this exercise, we also discovered that someone could always divine a key message from a piece of content that was otherwise not clear. Someone would say, "What this slide is really trying to say is . . . " and then proceed to articulate a point in a way that was certainly not obvious.

Here's an example to illustrate what I mean. Let's say this is the slide we are looking at:

Widget Sales

- 10% growth in Europe
  - Widgets sold 70% blue, 20% red, 10% orange
- North America sales declining
  - 50% decline in red widgets sold, 30% uptick in blue, orange sales flat
- Asia/Pacific 50% growth
  - Widgets sold 95% blue, 4% red, 1% orange

In reviewing a slide like this, someone might say, "What this slide is really trying to say is . . . blue widgets are our best seller and we need to double down our efforts on them."

When we found key ideas that were nowhere to be seen on the original slide but were obviously some of the most important pieces of information, we'd write down the idea—"blue widgets are our best seller"—and flag it as a key idea as we continued to empty the pantry.

There is a song entitled "One Great Thing" by the legendary Scottish band Big Country. This song is the inspiration behind a question that can forever help you simplify word-heavy slides: "What's the *one great thing* this slide is trying to say?"

Here's the point: When you find yourself with an overwhelming amount of information to pull from, don't stress; just empty the pantry onto paper or a whiteboard and allow yourself to view all of the information together in one place. You will find that you have everything you need for your presentation and can start organizing the content and identifying the key points that will help you accomplish your goal. You will start to see patterns and relationships between your ideas that help you create an aMM-Mazing structure.

EXPLORE IDEAS FOR YOUR HOOK

You also need to think about a hook to grab your audience's attention, create a deeper impression, and help your audience understand why your presentation is important to them. As we discussed in Chapter 2, you have several options for compelling hooks. Here's the list again as a reminder:

- Analogies
- Quotes from a famous person or a customer
- Stories or anecdotes
- Customer case studies
- Statistics
- Rhetorical questions
- News articles

If you already have more information than you feel the presentation time allows for, including something as seemingly ancillary as a quote, story, statistic, or analogy might seem unnecessary.

After all, when you have your goal firmly in mind, you are focused on what your audience needs to hear rather than what you want to say. However, the hook can be the most powerful part of your presentation because it helps frame all of the detail you are going to say, helps your audience gain a deeper appreciation for why this information is relevant to them, and helps motivate your listeners to action.

What about humor?

I get this question a lot: "When I'm writing presentations, should I include some jokes?" Here's the principle I apply:

Unplanned, spontaneous humor is the best.

Unless you are literally writing a stand-up comedy routine or are gifted with natural rib-tickling facial expressions and have an incredible sense of comic timing, writing jokes into your presentations can spell disaster.

If you do want to include some planned jokes, you must be prepared for what to do when (not if) no one laughs. I have been both holding the mic and sitting in the audience when planned comedy went horribly wrong.

My wife once attended a huge corporate event where the presenter projected some Dilbert comic strips, paused while everyone read them, and waited for the audience to break out into peals of laughter. When people didn't actually laugh out loud, the presenter got visibly irritated with the audience, saying things like, "Oh, come on, that's funny! Why is no one laughing?" What a cringe-fest! I personally find Dilbert funny, but more in a dry, quietly amusing way. Expecting—even demanding—your audience to laugh is sure to make everyone feel awkward.

Remember that some people are offended by everything, so if you want to include something you find funny, expect that some members of the audience will probably be offended. If you think that you've found something completely unoffensive and amusing and want to include it, don't wait for laughs. When your punch line lands like a lead balloon, move on.

I've read plenty of session reviews, however, where audience members have commented favorably on humor. People appreciate enthusiasm and warmth, and when a presenter really engages with the audience, there's often spontaneous comedic moments that make the presentation sparkle.

So yes, humor can be good, but I've found that unplanned, spontaneous humor is the best. Funny or warm moments often happen naturally when you are well prepared, comfortable, and feel a good connection with your audience.

STEP 2. ARRANGE INTO THE RULE OF THREE

Equipment: Same as Step 1

People Involved: Same as Step 1

Tools: JAM Session Writing Process Checklist

Now that you have gathered everything you could possibly include, it's time to start arranging it into the basic structure of your presentation.

ORGANIZE YOUR PRESENTATION STRUCTURE

On the whiteboard or paper, create three "buckets" for your presentation structure, one for each part of your presentation: introduction, body, and conclusion. Next, transpose your key ideas into each of these buckets. It's easy to figure out what information will be included in your introduction and conclusion—everything else should be in the "body bucket" (why does that sound like something from a horror film?!). This is the first application of the rule of three.

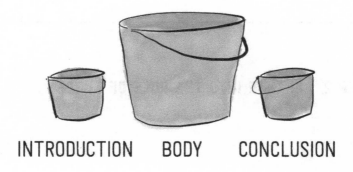

INTRODUCTION   BODY   CONCLUSION

ARRANGE THE BODY INTO THREE TOPICS

Every good presentation-training resource will tell you that it's a good idea to distill your information into three key ideas. This is a perfect example of the cliché "easier said than done." Knowing that you *should* do it and knowing *how* to do it are two very different things.

UNORGANIZED IDEAS   IDEAS ORGANIZED INTO THREE PARTS   BODY ORGANIZED INTO THREE TOPICS

Here are the methods that I use to identify the three key ideas around which I will structure my content within the body of my presentation. Sometimes I use only one of these, and sometimes I'll use a combination until I like the direction the presentation is going.

1. One-minute method
2. Restock the pantry method
3. Use a hack method

The One-Minute Method

Answer this: If your presentation was only one minute long, what would you say to accomplish your goal?

This can be an effective method to use because it draws your attention to the most compelling points out of everything gathered during your brainstorming session. Sometimes you will think of something entirely new or articulate something in a way that didn't come to mind as you "emptied the pantry."

If you still have the attention of the group who assisted you in your brainstorming session, ask each person in the room, "If you had one minute to talk to this audience, what would you say?" Write down each person's response. If this goes well, you will end up with two potential scenarios:

1. There's obvious consistency between all responses, and it's easy to identify three key ideas to build your presentation around.

2. Each person identified different things, but it's easy to group or consolidate these into three higher-level ideas.

However, if each person has different or conflicting thoughts as to what the three most important ideas are, you'll end up driving into the ditch of endless pontification. Don't stay there too long because it will drive you crazy.

If the one-minute method does not help you identify three key ideas to arrange your content around, it might be time to try another technique.

Restock the Pantry Method

This is a methodical way to identify the three main points in the body of your presentation. Earlier, we used the analogy "empty the pantry" when it comes to identifying important information from existing content. Once you've emptied an actual pantry, you quickly find yourself consolidating duplicates and throwing away old stuff. But what happens next?

You need to restock the pantry!

The chances are good that you are not going to just throw everything back in willy-nilly, but you are going to organize your goods in a system that you hope you will remember. You might arrange all of your food by type: Mexican, Italian, Chinese, and Thai, for example. But what if you only had three shelves? Then you would have to group everything a different way. In that case, you might group things into cans and jars, dried foods, and bottles.

It's the same idea when grouping information together to find your three points. If you imagine your presentation as a pantry that has only three shelves, it forces you to start organizing your information into only three topics.

As you start grouping like ideas together, you might find that they naturally end up in three groups. If so, fantastic! If you find more than three groups, you might be able to group your groups together into higher-level ideas, or you might have to organize differently until you come up with three main points. If you only "allow" yourself to have three main points, you will make it work, just the same as you would still restock your pantry in the most sensible way possible if you only had three shelves.

After you've come up with your three groupings, you might find that you are left with a few points that don't seem to fit in any group. If so, you can ask yourself, "Do these points really belong in this presentation?" If that happens, you may be able to comfortably discard them, or they might end up being great additions to your introduction or conclusion. If there's a lot of essential information that doesn't fit into any of your three categories, you may need to rethink your high-level groupings and come up with a new set.

If you still cannot come up with a satisfying or sensible group of three topics, try another method.

Use a Hack Method

If you are still struggling to identify three concepts to build your presentation around, here are a few examples of methods that I've used over the years. Think of them as hacks to help structure your information or to provide inspiration for arranging your material.

You could group your key ideas as points in time, such as past, present, and future. There are several ways to apply this:

Option 1	Option 2	Option 3
Past	Where we've been	How we got here
Present	Where we are	Current state
Future	Where we're going	Ideal future state

Or you might like to arrange your ideas in a combination of the "who, what, why, when, how" words. I've often used this breakdown:

1. Why this is important

2. What this means

3. How we can change

Or I establish the *why* in my introduction and then structure the body of my presentation around the details, like this:

Section 1: Intro: Why this is important

Section 2: Body

1. What we need to do
2. How we should do it
3. When we need to do it

Section 3: Conclusion: Next Steps

There is no correct answer for how you should arrange your material into three key points. The only rule I make for myself is to insist on having an introduction, a body, and a conclusion and on building the body around three topics.

DO A SANITY CHECK

The rule of three is art *and* science. As I covered earlier, the concept of people absorbing and remembering information, when presented in threes, has certainly been supported by scientific research. However, coming up with three main points in your presentation is an art. It takes effort and creative thinking to consolidate everything you need to say into three main ideas, and then into the three sections of your presentation.

I've often seen presenters choose three ideas, start building out their presentation, and then doubt that they are on the right path. Try not to overthink your three ideas once you've settled on them because that can drive you into another ditch where you stop making progress. If you start to doubt that your three key ideas are the right ones, change them only if a better structure springs to mind. If you don't have any better ideas, keep going! Even if your three-part structure isn't perfect, it will still be better than stalling out or presenting a ten-part agenda.

A word of encouragement: I have written thousands of presentations, and I have always been able to organize the core content into three topics. Sometimes they come quickly; sometimes they take several attempts. In the end, though, it's worth the effort because you can enjoy presenting your information in a simple, memorable way.

Look at the table of contents for this book and you'll see the various ways that I arranged the material within this book.

The *main structure* of this book is as follows:

1. Theory

2. Structure

3. Writing

Then, within the theory section, I arranged the material into these parts:

1. Meaningful

2. Memorable

3. Motivational

Within the structure section, the material is arranged the following way:

1. Introduction

2. Body

3. Conclusion

And in this section on writing, the concept is to JAM:

1. Jot everything down (which we are considering right now)

2. Articulate your words

3. Make your presentation tools

Yes, it's easier said than done, but I'm certainly not going to present advice that I'm not going to follow myself!

STEP 3. SCRIPT YOUR WORDS

3. Script

Equipment: A desktop or laptop computer

People Involved: Just the presentation writer

Tools (See Appendix):

❑ aMMMazing Outline Template

❑ JAM Session Writing Process Checklist

At this point, you should have a good understanding of the order of your material. You have arranged your information into your introduction, body, and conclusion, and you have identified your three main points, or sections, within the body.

Now it's time to transition from drawing tools to typing tools. This is when you can start to get logical in your thought process as you begin to type up everything so far.

This part is much faster and easier to do alone than with a group.

Don't be afraid of the concept of a script. We will not use a script when we present; we will simply use a script as a vehicle to help us move through the writing process. **First though, we will create an outline to see how all the ideas fit together.**

CREATE YOUR OUTLINE

To create your outline, you basically type up everything that you arranged in the previous step and tidy it up, and you will start to see your presentation taking shape. Use this template as the format of your outline:

aMMMazing Presentation Outline Template

INTRODUCTION

Attention-grabbing opening statement. Why this topic matters to your audience. Your hook. The introduction of your three key points.

BODY

KEY IDEA/TOPIC 1

    Supporting point 1

      Additional detail

    Supporting point 2

      Additional detail

    Supporting point 3

      Additional detail

KEY IDEA/TOPIC 2

    Supporting point 1

      Additional detail

    Supporting point 2

      Additional detail

    Supporting point 3

      Additional detail

KEY IDEA/TOPIC 3

    Supporting point 1

      Additional detail

    Supporting point 2

      Additional detail

    Supporting point 3

      Additional detail

CONCLUSION

Summary of key points. Refer to your hook from the introduction, perhaps with additional detail in light of what you have covered. Allow time for Q&A. Next steps for your audience and additional resources.

You'll notice that the template shows the information within each of the key ideas arranged into three supporting points. This is an extra step that can help you organize and simplify your thoughts within each subsection, but you don't have to get too crazy with grouping things into threes. The most important application of the rule of three is to have three main ideas or topics that your presentation is arranged around.

Once you've organized your information into an outline, it's a good idea to take a step back and review it to make sure there's a good flow between each section and idea. Here are a few questions you should ponder as you look at your outline:

- Does the overall flow work? Should anything be reworded or rearranged?

- If someone else reviewed the outline, would it make sense to them? If not, why not?

- Would the outline make a good one-page summary for a handout? If not, what is it missing?

Once you are happy with your outline, **save it** so that you can come back later to use it to create your handout. Copy your outline into a new document and then start turning it into a script.

WRITE A DRAFT SCRIPT

Now it's time to turn your outline into words.

Think about how to say what you want to say by putting some "meat on the bones" of your script. In this step, you will start to add in the "connective tissue" between your ideas and sections and begin writing specific phrasing you would like to use.

You are creating a first draft here. That's key. Don't overthink this step or try to get everything 100 percent perfect. We are taking a giant leap forward by beginning to craft the overall flow of the presentation and getting some ideas for phrasing down on paper. Most of the refining happens in the next major writing phase, "Articulate Your Words." Just get writing and let your words flow into the document!

You may not love the idea of scripting a presentation out word for word, especially when the goal is to deliver your content with a natural, engaging delivery. I totally get it. You might wonder, if you are not going to use a script when you actually present, why should you create one at all?

Returning to our songwriting analogy, there's a similarity between song lyrics and the wording of your presentation. Song lyrics are generally concise, usually poetic, and very often paint vivid word pictures. You don't need to be a poetry major to write a great presentation, of course, but you should strive to be succinct and colorful with your words, as if you were writing a song. This is especially true during the introduction, the transitions between topics, and the conclusion.

Select careful and deliberate phrasing for your most important points, as purposeful words can make them stand out. When you paint vivid word pictures with well-worded analogies, stories, and examples, you can make a deep impression on your audience.

If you do this well, you can strike your listeners' imaginations even without a slide deck. And if you are using a slide deck, you'll make your job of creating visuals much easier because you've already painted mental images that you can reinforce with actual images.

Sometimes I'll type out an entire presentation just to see if it all makes sense. Sometimes I will only write down a few specific phrases that I want to include. If you decide not to create an entire script, at least write down some phrasing for the following elements of the presentation.

- **Introduction**

Script an attention-grabbing opening statement. Give thought to how and when you would introduce yourself (if this is necessary) and introduce your key points. If you are using an analogy, write down some specific words for how you will introduce and explain it to make sure that it makes sense.

- **Conclusion**

I like to revisit my introductory words in my conclusion, often restating the exact same phrase or quote I started with, so I'll often write my concluding comments while I'm writing my introduction. Think about the words you will use in your concluding statement. Ask yourself if your conclusion is as well crafted as your introduction.

- **Linking Statements**

Carefully choose statements that will link your sections or ideas together so that your audience is able to follow your logic (especially if you are using an analogy or story throughout your presentation). If you are using an analogy, it's important to spell out the relationship between your analogy and your subject matter. Otherwise, your audience may get lost.

At this point, you'll have written your draft script. Your words will continue to be refined throughout the next steps, so don't worry if it seems too long at this point or if you aren't entirely happy with it—you are only one-third of the way through the writing process.

Stuck? Go back to the drawing board!

While I always brainstorm using paper or whiteboards (See Steps 1 and 2), I will transition to a computer to type up my ideas and create my script (Step 3). Many times, I have been typing away, creating my script, and then got stuck. Perhaps something new occurred to me that completely altered the flow or order of my information, or a detail sprang to mind about my analogy that drastically altered how I was going to use it.

When I find myself typing and retyping and ordering and reordering information in a document on my computer, and I realize that I'm no longer making progress, I see it as a sign that I need to think the content out more. I'll go back to the drawing board and allow myself time to think through the ideas again on paper. It's incredible how doing that can help refocus your mind and let you come up with new ideas.

WHAT NOT TO SAY

If you are not yet convinced as to why specific and deliberate wording matters, and you are tempted to stick to a "grab the mic and see what comes out approach," I'd like to share a few examples of things said during presentations that have had unfortunate outcomes. Not to be dramatic, but I've come to accept that even one unfortunately worded phrase can undermine your whole presentation.

While I've heard (and said) a lot of cringey statements (that I wish I could have taken back as soon as I said them) at all points of my presentations, I'm going to focus this discussion on words heard during the introduction. These examples illustrate how important it is to craft your opening words carefully.

Here are some actual statements made in presentations that should have never been uttered:

"I'm about to present ninety minutes of content in sixty minutes."

These were the opening words of a keynote presenter at a marketing conference I attended. The presenter was obviously trying to excuse the volume and pace of information the audience was about to be subjected to, right up front.

It's a curious feeling when you feel overwhelmed and underwhelmed at the same time. I felt overwhelmed before he even got into the rest of his presentation, because he told me I was about to feel that way. I felt underwhelmed because it appeared that he had not put much effort into preparing the presentation for this event.

This is the modern-day equivalent of the famous adage "I'm sorry this letter is so long; I didn't have time to make it shorter." In a personal letter, a phrase like that is warm and endearing and includes a sense of urgency. It seems as if the writer wanted to get it to you so quickly that expediency excuses verbosity. However, as an introduction to a presentation, especially a keynote, it just sounds as though the presenter hasn't spent enough time preparing.

Personally, I'd much rather the speaker presented sixty minutes of excellent content in sixty minutes (or less), not ninety minutes of content crammed into sixty-plus minutes (it's no surprise that the presenter went over time).

Think about the entire point of this book and the core concept of arranging your information into three key ideas to help you accomplish the goal of your

Dear Audience,

I'm sorry this presentation is so long, I didn't have time to write a short one.

(Un)Kind Regards,

Your Presenter.

presentation. If the presenter had done this, he could have easily trimmed a ninety-minute presentation to sixty minutes, because he would have removed some of the ancillary detail supporting his key ideas while making the same important points.

I mean, if a presenter can't get the point across in sixty minutes (a whole hour!), then they probably don't really know what their point is at all.

"I was going to show you a demo but . . . "

It's painful when something that you planned to show your audience doesn't work. This could be a demo, video, or something else. While it's upsetting to you as the presenter, you do not have to share this emotion with your audience. When you say something like, "I wanted to show you X, but it isn't working," all that you accomplish is making your audience feel as though they missed out on something.

I've read plenty of session review surveys with statements like these: "The presenter's demo didn't work" and "It's a shame that we didn't get to see the demo." The only reason that the audience knew they missed out on something was because the presenter told them and put that thought in their heads. If the presenter had simply carried on with the presentation, covered the key ideas, and hadn't drawn attention to the things that failed, the audience would never have known that something didn't work as planned. The presenter would have been able to keep the attention of the audience focused on what they did see and hear rather than what they didn't.

DON'T ACCIDENTALLY UNDERMINE YOUR OWN CONTENT

Next are two examples when I made totally meaningless off-the-cuff comments that I regret saying. I'm sharing these so that you can avoid making the same mistakes!

"I promise it's not . . . "

I delivered a session at a software conference to show how the featured software worked in conjunction with a third-party software application. My intention was to show how the integration between the two applications could help the attendees overcome some of the challenges they faced in their own environments. The way I structured the presentation was like this:

Topic 1: The problems the primary software application solves

Topic 2: The problems the third-party application solves

Topic 3: The additional problems they solve when integrated

As I introduced my second topic, I made the throwaway statement, "Now, as I discuss the problems that the third-party software solves, I promise it's not a commercial for that product—we have no affiliation with them—but it's important to understand what benefits it provides before getting into the integration."

Guess what three separate people commented in their surveys? "It sounded like a commercial for the third-party application." Now, maybe I was a little too enthusiastic in extolling the benefits of that other software, but I firmly believe that I planted that idea in their minds because they used the exact same words that I gave them. It was frustrating to see that statement mentioned in the reviews because it proved they heard the opposite of what I was trying to say.

"You might think that this is not that valuable . . . "

In a technical training class, I presented troubleshooting advice for a specific issue that was very complex to diagnose. Over the years, I had been pulled into scores of tech-support calls on the topic, so I had become fairly knowledgeable on the underlying technology. Several issues that we encountered were so weird that, at times, we honestly thought there was no solution to the problem and we were (literally at times) banging our heads against the desk. In every case, though (usually by some kind of miracle), we eventually figured out the issue and documented the solution. After a few years of struggling with these issues, we realized that we had successfully resolved every possible scenario. We had *finally* mastered this problem and understood why every issue occurred.

I gathered all of the notes and documentation that we had and, after a lot of collaboration, created a simple one-page troubleshooting guide. We had created a foolproof tool to help anyone diagnose the issues by simply following the specific steps in a specific order. We were so excited about it, and I couldn't wait to share it with the class.

As I distributed the troubleshooting guide, I introduced it by saying, "Now, you might think that all we are about to do is walk through a one-page troubleshooting guide. But let me tell you, this is the end result of countless hours of troubleshooting these issues, and we've spent a long time developing and testing the methods here. This will save you hours of frustration . . . " and I continued extolling the benefits of this incredible tool we'd created.

Guess what a few people mentioned in their surveys? "All we did was walk through a one-page troubleshooting guide." When reading those comments, I felt like banging my head on my desk all over again! Yes, we did walk through a one-page troubleshooting guide, but the class also delivered on the stated promise and saved everyone in the room from countless hours of frustration trying to figure it out for themselves.

I realized later that my "you might think that all we are about to do is" comment undermined the value of what we had created and what I was about to share. I had inadvertently planted the idea in the heads of the audience that this wasn't going to be a valuable activity, and that was all some people remembered from the class. What a bummer!

In both cases, I didn't plan to introduce the topic the way I did, and those phrases just kind of came out. The next time I presented the same topics, I chose specific and deliberate wording to introduce the information exactly as I wanted. And guess what? In the session reviews there was no repeat of the sentiments previously mentioned.

The point is, you should avoid off-the-cuff statements in your introduction, avoid sharing your frustrations with the audience, and avoid setting the wrong tone before you begin.

If you use deliberate, carefully chosen, and well-rehearsed words for your introduction, you will avoid statements like the ones mentioned here and instead focus on captivating your audience.

8

THE *A* IN JAM: ARTICULATE YOUR WORDS

AT THIS POINT, WE'VE MADE a ton of progress toward our final presentation. In the *J* of the JAM process, we jotted down all of our ideas, structured them into an outline, and created an initial script. What comes next? *A* for Articulate! We'll speak through the whole thing!

As I discussed in the introduction to this section, I call this the JAM process because it goes back to a fundamental truth in songwriting: Songwriters do not write songs in silence. After coming up with lyrical or musical ideas, they play them out loud (or JAM!) to see what they sound like. Only upon hearing how their ideas sound individually and together can they decide what to keep, what to discard, and what to change—and then the song starts to take shape.

I'm sure you've heard people say "practice, practice, practice" when it comes to delivering presentations. When saying this, people are generally recommending the idea of practicing your presentation out loud. However, remember, we're not at the practicing stage yet—we are still in the writing process. Simply put: *You need to speak aloud while you are writing your presentation.*

This step may seem unnecessary, but it is not. When you say your presentation out loud, you will want to make changes. By embracing this fact, you can use this to your advantage rather than feeling frustrated that you are making changes after you thought you were done.

When you speak out loud, you will *hear* what your ideas sound like. You can observe how well your information flows (or doesn't) and how long it takes to cover everything you want. Then you can keep the things that sound good, ditch the things that don't, and change the things that need to be changed.

Steps 4, 5, and 6 make up the Articulate phase of the JAM process.

STEP 4: SPEAK OUT LOUD

Equipment: A quiet space where you can talk aloud comfortably, your printed script, a pen or pencil, and a timer

People Involved: Just the presentation writer

Tools: JAM Session Writing Process Checklist

Now it's time to hear what your presentation sounds like from beginning to end.

EMBRACE THE EMPTY ROOM

Talking to an empty room might feel strange at first, and you might feel a little self-conscious, but think about this: If you can't get over talking to empty chairs, how will you ever get comfortable talking to them when they are occupied?

But what if people walk past and look at you strangely when they see you talking to yourself? Who cares? It's better to have one or two people think that you are a bit odd than to have a whole room of people think the same thing as you fumble through your words out loud for the first time.

There is often a big disconnect between how words sound in our head and how they sound when we say them out loud. It's much better to experience the awkwardness of how your presentation sounds when you're talking to an empty room than to realize it doesn't sound right when you're in front of an audience and breaking into a cold sweat.

Sometimes, as I'm working on a presentation and talking through a section aloud, I'll realize that I am intensely bored by what I am saying. If I am boring myself, how can I expect my audience not to be bored too? When I feel like that, it's often a signal to me that I've included too much detail, and then I start trying to figure out what can be eliminated or changed.

EXPECT TO MAKE A LOT OF CHANGES

For the first read-through, simply read through your script aloud and time yourself to get a sense of how long the entire thing is.

The key to success in this step is to expect that you are going to want to make changes.

Many thoughts and ideas will spring to mind as you vocalize your script for the first time. Here are a few things that I regularly experience while I'm sounding out ideas for the first time:

- I stumble over phrasing, explanations, or even introductions that sounded simple in my head (or on paper), and I realize I need to figure out the right words to say.

- Specific phrasings for analogies spring to my mind that I love, and I want to work them into my presentation.

- While the order of the main points seemed to make logical sense on paper, it doesn't seem to flow well aloud, and I realize I need to reorder some of the sections.

- Sections of the presentation seem as though they are dragging on too long because there's way too much detail.

As you read your script aloud for the first time, take notes on changes and tweaks you want to make and for any new concepts that come to you. These are often the ideas that you will end up including in your final presentation.

TIME YOURSELF (BUT DON'T WORRY ABOUT TIMING TOO MUCH YET)

At the first read-through, let the timer run to see how long it takes from beginning to end. That will give you a general idea of how much you need to cut or add. Don't worry too much about your timing because you are still writing your presentation and working out your ideas. However, even at this stage, it's helpful to know if you are going to go way over or way under your allotted time.

STEP 5: DOCTOR YOUR SCRIPT

Equipment: A computer and your marked-up script

People Involved: Just the presentation writer

Tools: JAM Session Writing Process Checklist

Now it's time to revise, alter, or adapt your script based on the notes you scribbled down during your read-through.

BE RUTHLESS, NOT SENTIMENTAL

Your script will likely have information that seemed important at first but you've realized you can live without. Don't be sentimental over ideas that you initially liked. If they don't sound right or seem unnecessary now—get rid of them. Follow the advice of the first band I ever saw in concert, the Scottish rockers Del Amitri, and "Kiss This Thing Goodbye!"

BE HONEST

If, as you speak out loud, you realize some of your information sounds boring and dull, then change it. The whole point of following this methodology is to avoid BAD presentations, so be honest with yourself. Note the sections that need some help and change them.

GET CREATIVE

Look for ways to make your points more interesting or lively. Sometimes you can replace a lot of detail with a story or an analogy that will help you get the same point across in a much more compelling way. Get creative with ideas and include anecdotes, adages, stories, or analogies that may have sprung to mind as you talked through your script aloud.

STEP 6: REPEAT UNTIL HAPPY

Equipment: Space where you can talk aloud comfortably, your printed script, a pen or pencil, and a timer

People Involved: Just the presentation writer

Tools: JAM Session Writing Process Checklist

Now, talk through your script again and keep doctoring it until you are happy with it.

If you feel as if you've knocked it out of the park after one read-through—your phrasing was perfect and your timing was dead-on—then congratulations! You are ready to move on to the next step.

However, it's likely that you'll want to make some additional changes. If you do, read your script aloud again to see what it sounds like after your changes. It's very possible that you will need to do this several times until you like how it sounds and are within your allotted time limit.

KEEP CHIPPING AWAY

Writing presentations is like the process of carving a granite sculpture. At first, you have a rough outline, and as you work it into a script and then talk through it, the overall shape begins to emerge. As you continue talking aloud and refining your content, the rough ideas eventually turn into a smooth flow with clear details.

If you expect the process to be like sculpting a hard lump of information into something beautiful, you will enjoy it and make peace with the fact that each revision is a step closer to creating something excellent. If you don't expect that to happen, it's easy to feel frustrated and rush to the finish, where you end up with a rough final presentation.

Speaking of the word *rush*, one of my great inspirations is the late Neil Peart from the band Rush. Not only did he inspire me to try new things on the drums that I never thought possible, his clever use of lyrics in his songwriting continues to inspire me even when writing presentations—to incorporate clever word play and avoid clichés. One of Rush's songs is called "Carve Away the Stone," and I often hum this to myself when reworking the words in my presentations.

DON'T GET TOO ATTACHED TO YOUR SCRIPT

Don't spend any time editing your spelling, grammar, punctuation, or passive voice. You are not writing a document that others will read; you are composing a presentation that others will hear, and no one wants to hear a presenter reading word for word from a script.

We are using the script as a vehicle to organize our thoughts, to decide where we need specific phrasing, to get a sense of the overall flow, to mark where we need to make changes, and to figure out how long it will take to speak through from start to finish. You will eventually present without it, so don't get too attached to it!

At this point, I start doing "conversational" read-throughs. I imagine that I am standing in front of my audience and use my script as notes rather than reading it word for word.

PAY ATTENTION TO TIMING

As you begin weaning yourself from your script and timing your conversational read-throughs, you'll find yourself naturally adding phrases and pauses, and maybe even throwing in some new thoughts here and there. It's important to time yourself carefully.

If you find that you go way over time, then you are going to have to cut some content. A natural, engaging delivery is far more important than a rushed, rigid delivery just to get all of your points in.

When I go over time, I find that it's handy to time myself reading through each section individually. This helps me zero in on areas where I can cut information.

Once you are happy with your script and how it sounds, flows, and feels—congratulations! You have written your aMMMazing presentation!

9

THE *M* IN JAM: MAKE YOUR PRESENTATION TOOLS

AT THIS POINT, YOU HAVE composed an end-to-end presentation that you could deliver without projecting any slides.

Let that thought sink in for a second. You have composed an aMMMazing presentation without needing any graphics.

It's a pretty safe assumption, however, that most presentation scenarios today come with the expectation that you will use a slide deck. Graphics can complement and reinforce your words, lending them added power, so we will include the creation of your slides in this phase.

It's interesting that we usually spend the majority of our time creating the visuals that our audience will look at and the least amount of time on what we, as the presenter, will look at! It's no wonder that we feel nervous when we get up there and our minds go blank. You should put as much thought into your speaker notes—what they look like and how you will use them—as you do the visuals your audience will look at. Your presentation notes can make or break your delivery, so we will also include the creation of these (and discuss teleprompters) in this phase.

Providing your audience with a purposeful handout containing a summary of your key points (not just sending a copy of the slide deck) can add tremendous value to your presentation. This tactic can help you reinforce your key points, spur your audience to action, and set your presentation apart from the rest.

In this chapter, I'll show you how to create all three of these presentation tools: a great slide deck, simple speaker notes, and satisfying handouts.

If you are presenting without projecting any slides, however, skip Step 7 and go straight to Step 8 and focus on creating your slide notes and handouts.

STEP 7: VISUALIZE YOUR SLIDE IDEAS

Equipment: A pen or pencil and paper

People Involved: Just the presentation writer

Tools: aMMMazing Slide Deck Structure Template (See Appendix)

Which slide application is the best?

Microsoft PowerPoint often gets a bad rap. I, too, hate terrible PowerPoints that are full of words and should have been printed off and handed out, rather than just being read word for word from the screen. I've also seen some stunning PowerPoint slide decks that are perfect accompaniments to spectacularly crafted presentations.

When someone says that they hate PowerPoint, it's like saying that they hate record players because all they've ever heard are bad records. When I hear people saying that, I get knocked down. But I get up again.

Some people turn to applications that offer an alternative to traditional slide decks—such as Prezi, which allows the presenter to plot their visuals on a large canvas instead of linear slides—hoping that the variety in visual approach will make their presentation a little more interesting to their audience and help to differentiate them as a speaker.

Here's the harsh truth though: Simply moving a bad PowerPoint slide deck into a Prezi canvas usually results in a presentation that is both boring and dizzying.

I'm not knocking Prezi either, because I've seen some gorgeous presentations created in Prezi that were a true joy to behold.

Whatever your presentation weapon of choice, by creating your presentation first and your visuals second, you will be able to focus on using the tool for its intended purpose: to visually support and reinforce the words you are saying.

The analogy of songwriting helps to illustrate where you should spend most of your time as a presenter: crafting what people will *hear*. The visual accompaniment backs up your message, even making it more impactful, kind of like the music video.

If you stick to the principle that your visuals should be a simple and powerful visual accompaniment to your well-crafted words, it will help you put your focus in the right place—no matter what tool you use.

If you want to exponentially speed up the creation of your slide deck, create a storyboard by sketching your slide ideas on paper before you make them in your slideware application. This allows you to visualize exactly what your deck will look like before you create it.

I know this sounds like an extra step, but I have found it to be a massive time saver. When you use drawing tools to brainstorm ideas, you experience a free flow of thought and tap into your creative-thinking faculties much better than when you are working directly in a slideware application. Sketching your ideas on paper allows you to brainstorm slide ideas without worrying about how you are going to create your slides, what the perfect graphics look like, or where any existing slides or graphics reside that you might want to repurpose. Sketch first. Create later. It works.

Do this: Simply grab a piece of paper and create a bunch of boxes on it. Then, as you read through your script, sketch out a rough idea of the visuals you need to accompany your words. The process of "words first, visuals later" ensures that you are creating your slides to match your words, rather than trying to say words to match your slides. My office is full of slide deck sketches like the one on the next page.

You do not have to be an artist to do this! As you can see in the example, my sketches are extremely rough. I'll often write down "picture of a fast car" or "use X slide" without worrying about where to find the image or slide at that moment. Make sure to include your structural slides in your sketches too, noting where you will include your title, agenda, questions, and closing statement slides.

Before we get into the process of creating visuals, let's make clear what I am not recommending. I am not recommending that you take sentences from your script and copy them into slides. Your slides should be *graphical or pictorial* accompaniments to the

Presentation Deck

Karaoke

neon sign

Singing = Presenting

nervous presenter

Confident Presenter

vs ?

Even the most amazing Karaoke Singer in the world is not the person who wrote the song

YOU ARE THE COMPOSER

a MMMazing

① meaningful
② memorable
③ Motivahmal

Structure

What method do you use to compose presentations?

1. Who is Audience
2. What do they care about
3. What do you want them to do?

Audience

Boss   team Crowd

What care about?

Pick a verb, any verb

② memorable

Rule of 3

words that you will be saying. Your slides should not contain all of your words. Your slides should contain simple visuals, and the slide notes should contain your speaker prompts.

If your slides are full of the same words that you will say, what's the point of speaking? You may as well just distribute the slide deck and save everyone time. If your intention is to create beautiful slide decks to help you reinforce the words you have already prepared, then you should apply the following principles.

THE PLAYLIST OF AMMMAZING SLIDE DECKS

I'll share six principles to keep in mind as you sketch out your slide ideas. As we have been likening presentation writing to songwriting, let's examine these principles through songs. Here's the playlist for an aMMMazing slide deck:

SONG 1: "SIMPLE AND CLEAN" BY HIKARU UTADA

The title of this song, by Japanese-American songwriter Hikaru Utada, says it all. It's what all great slide decks should be—simple and clean. Many corporations use slide templates that are full of unnecessary visual clutter. Why does every slide need to contain a corporate or conference logo? Will people suddenly forget what meeting they are in if some of the slides don't have a logo? Why do the lines, swoops, or bubbles of a corporate brand have to appear in every slide? The simple answer is they don't! If your brand is so fragile that every slide in every presentation must remind people of it, then you might have bigger problems to address than can be fixed by any single presentation. Principle 1: *Keep your slides simple and clean.*

SONG 2: "MORE THAN WORDS" BY EXTREME

This classic '90s song proclaims that using more than words is all it takes to make it real, and the song is right. It's said that a picture is worth a thousand words. When you choose the right pictures to accompany your words, you can convey a much deeper meaning than your words alone. Try to replace as many words as you can with pictures, images, icons, diagrams, and photographs. Principle 2: *Use more graphics than words.*

SONG 3: "STATEMENTS" BY LOREEN

Your slides should *never* contain full paragraphs, unless it's a direct quote for a specific reason. If you do need to include explicit wording for some reason, use statements instead of paragraphs. Loreen proclaims "Statements!" in this song, and this is an excellent thing to keep in mind while creating your slides. Principle 3: *Use statements instead of paragraphs.*

SONG 4: "BULLET WITH BUTTERFLY WINGS" BY SMASHING PUMPKINS

Although this song is *clearly* not about creating slide decks, the title of this song provides a brilliant idea for what to do when you want to list some words on a slide—make them pretty! When you need to include a list of statements, instead of using boring bullet points, choose an icon to match your words. Iconography will make your slides look nicer and help you to convey a deeper meaning behind each statement. When listing a few ideas on a slide, you do not need to list them top to bottom. (Perhaps this was another idea seeded into the general public by the S.O.R.R.Y. Not S.O.R.R.Y. organization responsible for the corporate disease presentation.) Why not list your key points left to right with a statement beneath a well-chosen icon? Principle 4: *Use icons instead of bullet points.*

SONG 5: "THE PYRAMID" BY LOVE OF DIAGRAMS

It's the name of this Australian indie rock band that is the headline: Love of Diagrams. At the same time, the song title reminds us that shapes are nicer to look at than words and that visual cues can help us communicate deeper concepts than words alone. The shape of a pyramid, for example, can help us convey a simple relationship between three related ideas or a hierarchy of layered concepts that reach a peak. Processes, relationships, hierarchies, and other complex ideas should be illustrated visually for your audience. Don't just hope that they will be able to draw the comparison in their minds as they read the words. Principle 5: *Use diagrams instead of descriptions.*

SONG 6: "FILL IT UP" BY TRIBAL SEEDS
FT. GONZO & NEW KINGSTON

When inserting pictures into your slide deck, it's an excellent idea to remember this reggae song by Tribal Seeds. Look at all of your screen real estate and do what the song title says. Make your images, screenshots, and embedded videos *full screen.* Literally fill up the entire slide with your image! Don't be afraid, go for it! If you need to add words to the image, add them! If the letters end up blending into the image, experiment with the color of the text, or try adding solid or semi-transparent colors into the textbox, until you create the contrast you need. If you still are concerned that you are obscuring the slide template or corporate logo, replay the first song in the playlist! Principle 6: *Use full-screen graphics and screenshots.*

The six principles of aMMMazing slide decks:

Principle 1: Keep your slides simple and clean.

Principle 2: Use more graphics than words.

Principle 3: Use statements instead of paragraphs.

Principle 4: Use icons instead of bullet points.

Principle 5: Use diagrams instead of descriptions.

Principle 6: Use full-screen graphics and screenshots.

EXAMPLES APPLYING THE PRESENTATION PLAYLIST

Here are some examples of how to apply the six principles. Principles 1 and 2 are applied in each one, being simple and clean and utilizing more graphics than words. Let's look at some before and after examples:

Example A: Application of Principles 1, 2, and 3

There are so many considerations in what is most important to a company. We believe that, first and foremost, our success is thanks to the success of our people. That's what is most important.

Successful People = Our Success

Example B: Application of Principles 1, 2, and 4

Example C: Application of Principles 1, 2, and 5

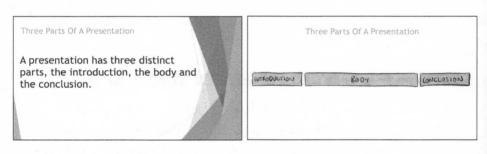

Example D: Application of Principles 1, 2, and 6

But wait! My slides *must* contain a lot of words, because I am using them as a handout.

I hear that all the time!

Here's a question I like to ask in return: "Do you want your slides to be an excellent presentation tool, or do you want them to be an excellent handout?" Because if they are both, they will not be good as either one.

Slide decks containing lots of words are not effective presentation tools because they visually overwhelm your audience with information. Your audience ends up reading what's on the screen and tuning out the words you are saying.

Conversely, slide decks with hardly any words and lots of visuals can be excellent presentation aids (visually supporting and reinforcing the words you are saying) but make terrible handouts because the audience will not be able to reference all of the detail you feel is important.

The answer? *Make your slide deck for your delivery. Make a handout to leave behind.*

Ask yourself: Would your audience rather wade through your entire slide deck after you leave, or would they prefer to review a clean one-page handout with your key ideas and most salient points highlighted? The answer should be obvious.

Try it immediately! Make a one-page handout for the next presentation you deliver.

When you follow the steps to writing an aMMMazing presentation, you'll see that creating a one-page handout is extremely easy to do. It will basically be the same as the outline from which you build your entire presentation and slide deck. Creating a handout becomes a simple by-product of your writing process.

Even if you don't have time to go back to the drawing board and follow the JAM process, challenge yourself to make a one-page handout for your next presentation. It's an interesting exercise to go through because it forces you to think through your material and identify what your most important points are! If you can't distill your most important information to one page, do you even know what your most important points are?

Many times, people tell me that when they try to do that—even without everything else in this book—they end up reordering and simplifying their entire presentation for the better!

STEP 8: MAKE YOUR VISUALS

Equipment: A computer, your presentation application of choice, and your sketches

People Involved: Just the presentation writer

Tools: aMMMazing Slide Deck Structure Template (See Appendix)

Now that we've sketched out what we want to make, it's time to put together the presentation materials. These are what your audience will look at, what you will look at, and what you will leave behind as a handout.

BUILD YOUR SLIDE DECK (IF YOU ARE USING ONE)

You've already created your words and considered the principles behind the slide deck playlist, and then sketched out a storyboard to match, so building your slide deck should go relatively quickly. When I get to this stage, I put on my headphones and blast some loud music. I find it hard to listen to music while I'm working through the steps leading up to this point because they all require me to *think*. But, in this stage of the JAM process, I'm not really thinking up anything new; I'm just creating the slides I need based on my storyboard. My slides are usually full-screen images, simple diagrams, quote slides, or simple phrases.

Once you've created your slides, paste the words from your script into the notes section for the corresponding slides. This is a good exercise to make sure that you have created the right slides for your talking points. Now you can put your script aside and stop using it because your words are now on your slide notes.

If you notice that there is a lot of text in the notes of one slide, that could indicate that you need to create another slide or two, depending on what you're saying. After you've done all of this, your slide deck is ready for rehearsal.

DECIDE HOW TO USE YOUR SPEAKER NOTES

Many presenters don't really think about what they will be looking at during a presentation until it begins, and they realize that they can't see the slides or their slide notes very well.

You need to decide what you will be looking at during your presentation and then plan accordingly.

Here are three presenter options. Which would you choose?

- **Option A:** View the same slides as your audience.
- **Option B:** Use the "presenter view" to refer to your slide notes.
- **Option C:** Read from a teleprompter or printed script.

I prefer Option A, hands down. This delivery method allows you to spend more time looking at your audience rather than your words, and results in a significantly more natural and engaging delivery. However, when the slide deck incorporates the six simple principles, there will not be a lot of words on the slides. That will force you to rehearse with your slides enough to ensure that you know exactly what you are going to say, how you are going to say it, and how long it's going to take you to say it. You need to rehearse enough to make sure that your words are firmly in mind before you present.

If you choose Option B or C, please remember this: You still need to practice with the tool you'll be using to present. If you have not practiced, it's extremely difficult to read word for word from slide notes or a teleprompter and sound natural.

If you are using the slide notes or a teleprompter, try to edit your script down to only the key phrases or bullet points. That will free you from being trapped into reading word for word, and you will be able to speak more naturally. As you practice, you will identify the sections where you are comfortable and know exactly what you are going to say, and the sections where you need to be reminded of specific wording. In the latter situation, make as many bullet points as you need. It's OK for you to look at tons of bullet points; it's not OK for your audience!

> **Word of caution:** If you are going to edit your script down to bullet points, do it well ahead of time and practice with your reduced script as you talk through it out loud.

I always talk through my presentations out loud while I'm writing them, and then again while I'm rehearsing them, so that I can speak naturally without relying on a word-for-word script. Several times, however, I've made the mistake of practicing with my full printed script in front of me and then reducing my script down to bullet points right before the presentation. When I've done that, I've found that I easily lose my place or forget what my bullet points mean because my new notes are totally unfamiliar to me.

The point is this: You need to create the tools that you will use as speaker notes in advance and practice until you are totally comfortable with them.

A Note About Teleprompters

A teleprompter can be a good tool to use, but like any tool, you need to learn how to use it to get the best out of it.

Personally, I will never use a teleprompter.

Yes, I know the State of the Union Address is delivered using a teleprompter, and the president reads it word for word. The audience expects this because a badly phrased sentence could start a world war or bomb the economy. As I'm sure you have noticed, some presidents have been able to do this expertly, sounding as though they were talking from the heart, and others . . . not so much.

continued

I have read many reviews of executive keynote presentations where the attendees complained that an executive "just read from a tele-prompter." That's brutal feedback for an executive who has been trying to inspire an audience. No executive wants that to be the takeaway from their big moment.

A full word-for-word script on a teleprompter or printed page can be a crutch to help you avoid falling flat on your face while you are up there. But if you've ever used literal crutches, you'll also know that the best a crutch can do is to help you limp along.

LOOK INTO MY EYES

If you do insist on using a teleprompter, the best advice I can give is to try to reduce your script down to bullet points or phrases, and then practice with your teleprompter as many times as you can before you deliver your presentation. If you have not practiced with the teleprompter and find your-self trying to follow it for the first or second time in front of an audience, it's really hard to look away from it while you are presenting.

I know, because I've tried. A teleprompter can be like Medusa's stare that you can't escape from, turning you to stone in front of your audience.

CREATE YOUR HANDOUT

If you have followed the steps so far, you have already created the basis for a great handout: your outline. Now it's time to revisit it and turn it into a summary of your presentation.

You've likely rearranged and reworded some of your content as you adjusted your thoughts throughout each step, so you might need to adjust your outline based on those changes.

Simply pull up your outline, put it in your corporate tem-plate, clean it up, revise it based on the progress you've made, and voila—you have just created a killer one-page handout with all of your key points on it.

It really can be that easy when you follow the JAM process.

Can't I just give people my whole deck as a handout?

I've already addressed the concept that a slide deck cannot be both a great presentation tool and a great handout. But let's discuss this further by exploring the popular notion of providing the entire slide deck as a handout, with space to take notes on each page.

Over the years, I've probably been handed hundreds of printed slide decks (sometimes with a free binder!). When you receive one of these delights, how many pages do you actually take notes on? A few, perhaps, but you are certainly not taking notes on every single page. Not only is it a colossal waste of paper and money, but it's also really annoying to flip back through all of those pages to find the one or two where you wrote down something interesting.

Also, when you hand out your entire slide deck before you begin, your audience will inevitably flip ahead. That can make it hard for you to hold their attention and to build anticipation for your key points and ideas.

Perhaps the same secret society that infected corporations with the "corporate disease" slide deck also designed the function within slideware applications to be able to print them as handouts.

Your audience should take notes, and it's fantastic when they do because it means that you are saying things they want to remember. But they can take notes on a blank page or their mobile device or laptop just as well.

It's also extremely satisfying to see your audience taking notes when you know you are going to give them a beautiful one-page summary of all of the key points you want them to remember.

continued

Note, however, that for training classes or deeper technical presentations, a one-page handout is not enough. You may need to give your audience a workbook, a checklist, or a more detailed handout for them to understand, absorb, and remember certain details.

The key point is this though: Rather than merely printing your slide deck, spend the time and effort to create something purposeful to accompany your presentation.

STEP 9: SPEAK AND TWEAK

9. Speak

Equipment: Your slide deck, an empty room with a projector, and a slide clicker

People Involved: Just the presenter (assuming the presentation writer and the presenter are one and the same person!)

Tools: aMMMazing Presentation Evaluation Checklist (See Appendix)

You are almost there! But this "Speak" does not refer to the delivery. This is the final step of the *writing process* when everything comes together—your visuals and your slide notes—and you run through everything to understand what final changes you need to make.

SPEAK: PROJECT YOUR SLIDES, USE YOUR SLIDE NOTES, AND SAY YOUR PRESENTATION OUT LOUD

Do a complete, timed run-through with your slides, projector, clicker, and slide notes. As you talk and click through each slide, evaluate the following:

- How does the presentation look and sound?

- What is your timing?

- How does the presentation feel? Are there any areas that drag or areas where you can't remember the words?

TWEAK: EXPECT TO MAKE CHANGES

Sometimes at this point, as I speak through my presentation using only my slides or notes, I often find that I exceed the time available. When this happens, I usually think of a song by my favorite band of all time, Scottish Celtic rockers Runrig—"Something's Got to Give." I realize that I'm going to have to remove *something*—slides, stories, or examples—to make sure I end on time.

Even at this late stage, you will find things that you want to change, reorder, or simplify. Make changes to your phrasing, flow, and slides and run through the presentation again, until you are satisfied with your end product and your timing is ideal.

That last bit is important. Before you present, you should know exactly how long your presentation is down to the minute. Don't leave your timing to chance. Continue making changes and revising until you can deliver your entire presentation within the time limits of your presentation. Once you are happy with your words, your slides, and your timing, congratulations! You have written an aMMMazing presentation and created the visuals to go along with it.

REHEARSE

Going back to our song analogy, now that the writing work is over, are you ready for the live performance? Perhaps!

A songwriter might be ready to show up at an open mic night to give an airing of new songs for some feedback, without worrying too much about the performance being perfect. On the other hand, if they are going to be playing at a huge concert event before a large audience, they may need to go through several rounds of rehearsal.

So, depending on the occasion for which you are presenting, you might be ready to perform at this point, or this might be the start of your rehearsals.

If I am composing an important presentation, I'll invite others to a rehearsal so that I can get their feedback, but only after I'm happy with what I've created.

A rehearsal is usually as close to my final deliverable as I can make it. It's a great idea to ask someone to use the aMMMazing Presentation Evaluation Checklist (See the Appendix) to help identify any areas you should pay attention to. I use that checklist to ensure that I have incorporated all of the best techniques possible, and I often find things that I've overlooked.

A DRY RUN OR A REHEARSAL?

Do you organize meetings, events, or conferences? If so, scheduling time for the presenters to deliver their "final" presentations to a small group for feedback, prior to the event, is a great idea.

Many people use the term *dry run*. I prefer *rehearsal*. Here's why:

Dry run	Rehearsal
Sounds boring	Sounds grand
Carries no expectation	Carries the expectation of being almost ready
Evokes images of a meeting room	Evokes images of a theater

Seriously, who wants to listen to something dry? I have attended enough dry runs to know that the term itself carries very little expectation. Often, the presenter shows up unprepared and uses the time as a brainstorming session. The term *rehearsal* carries significantly weightier expectations, both for the presenter and for those invited along to provide valuable feedback.

One theory as to the origin of the term *dry run* comes from military training in the 1940s, where recruits handled unloaded (dry) guns in training, doing a "dry run." When they were finally allowed to fire their weapon, this was called a "wet run." Sounds gross. This also got me wondering if there is a relationship between dry runs and bullet points. Who would have figured that presentation clichés with roots in weaponry would end up being so *boring?*

You might then wonder, *How often do I need to rehearse?* The answer is easy: Rehearse until you are comfortable. You might be comfortable after one run-through, or you might need to run through your presentation several times.

Often people will comment to experienced presenters, "You are so natural up there" or "You make it look so easy!" Most of the time, the presenters who get these comments are those who rehearsed the most—in their offices, in hotel rooms, in the shower, while driving, or anywhere that they could speak out loud.

It takes a lot of effort to make a presentation seem easy, but it's worth it.

Now, you are ready to *perform* your presentation!

The JAM Process vs. a Live Jam Session

The nine steps in the JAM process ensure that you are as prepared as you can possibly be and that you know exactly how long your presentation is before you start speaking—allowing you to present your material with confidence.

Not all presentations are equal in relative importance, so you can flex the time you spend on each step according to the situation.

However, perhaps you are still thinking, *This all still seems like too much.* Maybe the idea of pulling some slides together and just "talking to them" feels like less up-front work and more exciting for you.

In that case, instead of using the JAM process, you are going to use your presentation time as a live, impromptu jam session.

I've played in many bands and have attended many gigs, and I've come to this realization—the only people who really enjoy long, live jam sessions are the ones in the band (and drunk people).

For the record, I really like the Dave Matthews Band, which is famous for long, lingering jam sessions live on stage. However, even these talented fellas are typically extrapolating well-structured songs that they have already written and recorded. They do not just show up and throw up a whole set list of untried ideas.

It's true that live jam sessions can be great and inspiring when performed by true musical virtuosos, but even these musical geniuses eventually have to get off the stage.

Even if you decide to stick to a mostly spontaneous delivery, the principles of the JAM process can help you do so while accomplishing the goals of your presentation within the time available.

SUMMARY OF THE JAM SESSION WRITING PROCESS

IN THIS SECTION, WE WALKED through the JAM process for writing presentations and delved into the three steps in each phase.

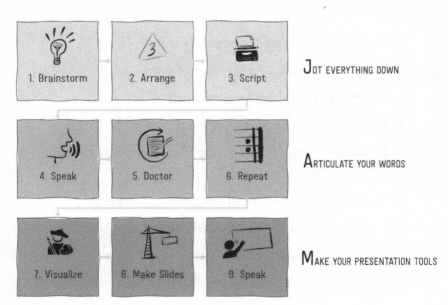

1. Brainstorm 2. Arrange 3. Script — **J**OT EVERYTHING DOWN

4. Speak 5. Doctor 6. Repeat — **A**RTICULATE YOUR WORDS

7. Visualize 8. Make Slides 9. Speak — **M**AKE YOUR PRESENTATION TOOLS

Would you like an easy way to remember the order of the nine steps? What's the backbone of a good song? Isn't it a steady beat?

Well, the first letters of these nine steps spell out something you need for a rock-solid song: **BASSDRVMS**.

And yes, I know the word "drum" has a *U* instead of a *V*, but this is rock and roll, baby! You can make up your own rules!

These BASSDRVMS will provide a solid backbeat to follow as you compose your presentations:

1. **B**rainstorm ideas and empty the pantry.

2. **A**rrange your ideas into the rule of three.

3. **S**cript a draft of the presentation.

4. **S**peak through the script out loud.

5. **D**octor your script based on the ideas that come to mind when you hear it out loud.

6. **R**epeat Steps 4 and 5 until you are happy with it.

7. **V**isualize your slide ideas by sketching a storyboard.

8. **M**ake your visuals, speaker notes, and handouts.

9. **S**peak and tweak until happy with your final presentation.

CONCLUSION

NOW YOU HAVE EVERYTHING YOU need to create your own aMMMazing presentations.

In Section 1, we covered presentation theory and tips to make your presentations *meaningful, memorable,* and *motivational.*

In Section 2, we delved into the secrets of structure and explained the key ingredients required to make your introduction meaningful, the main body of your content memorable, and your conclusion motivational.

In Section 3, we outlined the JAM session writing process and the nine steps to follow to create your words, visuals, and speaker notes.

In the Appendix, you will find tools that accompany all of the key points covered in this book, in a format you can use for reference as you compose your presentations.

Before you go, here are a few final thoughts.

AIM TO BECOME A PROLIFIC PRESENTATION WRITER

Have you heard the term "one-hit wonder"? It refers to an artist who has been successful with one hit song but has never quite been able to replicate it. It's not that they only wrote one song; it's just that only one song was deemed successful.

My goal is to ensure that you are not a "one-hit wonder" presenter, where you peak with the creation of a single presentation. Instead, you should aim to develop your writing style over time so that you can consistently create aMMMazing presentations. Consider yourself a presentation writer rather than just someone who presents. Commit to honing your craft and developing your own writing style and process. If that's your mindset, you'll always be looking for ways to improve the next presentation you create over the one you just delivered. You'll always be looking for new ideas and inspiration with the words you craft.

This is really the whole point of the songwriting analogy. There are artists out there who have become prolific songwriters, writing multiple hit songs sometimes for themselves, sometimes for other people. Taylor Swift and Ed Sheeran come to mind as people who have written a catalog of hits. Did you know that Ed Sheeran also wrote the One Direction song "Little Things," a chart-topping hit in multiple countries? Going a bit more old school, did you know that Prince (another prolific songwriter) wrote the Bangles' hit song "Manic Monday"? Did you know that Simple Minds (who have penned some of my all-time favorite songs) didn't actually pen the '80s classic "Don't You (Forget About Me)" themselves? Instead, it was written by Keith Forsey, who also cowrote songs for the movies *Ghostbusters*, *Beverly Hills Cop*, and *The NeverEnding Story*.

What I like most about the analogy of songwriting as it relates to presentation writing is that both are continual processes. Don't expect the next presentation you create, or every presentation, to be perfect and blow people's minds. Just like songwriting, sometimes you'll write a "hit," sometimes you'll write an "album track" or a "B-side" (I'm dating myself!), and sometimes you'll write a flop that you never want to hear again.

People who write songs for a living are never finished with their craft—they continue to write, improve, and evolve as tastes and trends shift. It's the same for you. So keep writing and keep experimenting, and pretty soon you'll find that you can write aMMMazing presentations consistently.

FIND THE TIME TO BE A COMPOSER

You might be wondering where you are supposed to find the time to follow all of these steps while you are doing your job and possibly working on several presentations and other projects at the same time.

The fact is this: All presentations take time to create; there is no getting around it. Creating an aMMMazing presentation doesn't necessarily take any longer than creating a boring and dull one—it's all about maximizing your time to make the biggest impact. Rather than spending hours shuffling slides around in silence, you can use the steps in this book to spend more time crafting the words first. That will significantly reduce the time spent within your slideware application. There's an old adage attributed to Abraham Lincoln where he apparently said, "If you give me six hours to chop down a tree, I'll spend the first four sharpening the axe." That is exactly how to think of this process. It doesn't take more time, but it helps you use your time more wisely and effectively and makes your presentations have much more impact when you deliver them—like swinging a very sharp axe.

If you commit to making every presentation as meaningful, memorable, and motivational as possible, then you must carve time out of your schedule to do all of the steps necessary to get there. Waiting until the last minute puts you under pressure, which can crush your ability to answer all of the necessary questions, think creatively and critically about your content, and take the steps necessary to create something of value.

When I receive a presentation assignment, I start working on it right away. I start a page or a file for the presentation, dump in everything I know, and then make sure I add information and ideas as they come to mind. Next, I reserve slots on my calendar to work on each specific task as far in advance as my schedule allows, and then I make sure I allow time to perform each step.

In fact, don't tell anyone, but I use the same structure in every presentation I write. I simply plug in the pieces I need. Using this process, I've helped to develop hundreds of presentations on topics that I've started off knowing very little about. But I do know the right questions to ask, the right techniques to apply, and how to structure the information to make it meaningful, memorable, and motivational.

Using the concepts in this book, I have been able to expedite my own writing process significantly. Even so, I never start writing at the last minute, if I can help it.

FINDING THE RIGHT BALANCE

While we should always strive to create meaningful, memorable, and motivational presentations, it's good to acknowledge that not all presentation scenarios are equal in importance or gravity. The principles and rules in this book apply to every presentation scenario, but how much time you should reasonably spend on each will differ. You have to find that balance.

It's not about the size of your audience or the length of the presentation; it's about how important the information is to you and your audience. When I have a presentation I deem really important (such as a presentation at an event or an executive meeting), I will *slow jam*, meaning I will plan to spend significant time on each of the nine steps to make sure I'm thoroughly ready. However, if my presentation is more of an update to a smaller team, I'll *speed jam*. I'll still follow the JAM process but move through each step more quickly.

Let's conclude by revisiting our opening question from the Introduction and add an additional choice:

How do you feel when you are standing before the mic and about to begin speaking in front of a room full of people?

Which of the following best describes you?

- ❏ Nervous
- ❏ Excited
- ❏ Terrified
- ❏ Energized
- ❏ Sweaty
- ❏ Confident in what you have written
- ❏ All of the above

If you would now check either of the last two boxes, then this book has accomplished its purpose.

In writing this book, I wanted you to have the knowledge and tools to help you write your own aMMMazing presentations that will captivate your audience. We've spent a lot of time covering the concepts of the three *M*'s: meaningful, memorable, and motivational. If you follow them, then you will also be able to deliver on the other part of the aMMMazing concept—your presentations will also have a little "zing"!

ammmazing!

APPENDIX:
TOOLS AND
TEMPLATES

AMMMAZING JAM SESSION WRITING PROCESS CHECKLIST

USE THIS CHECKLIST TO COMPLETE the steps for composing your presentations. For important presentations, slow jam—plan to spend significant time on each step. If you don't have much time, speed jam—move through the same steps more quickly.

JOT EVERYTHING DOWN

1. Brainstorm ideas

☐ Who is your target audience? What do you want them to do? What do they need to know?

☐ Empty the pantry—extract ideas from existing content.

☐ Explore ideas for your "hook"—an analogy, story, quote, statistic, news item, question.

2. Arrange into the rule of three

☐ Group related information and ideas into your introduction, body, and conclusion.

☐ Arrange the body around three main ideas.

☐ Do a sanity check (will the three main ideas really resonate with the audience?).

3. Script a draft

☐ Type up ideas to create a clean outline (save a simple outline for Step 8).

☐ Fill in specific wording for your introduction, linking statements, and conclusion.

☐ Add as much text as you'd like to complete your draft script.

ROUGH

ARTICULATE YOUR WORDS

4. Speak out loud

☐ Find a quiet space and read it aloud, start to finish.

☐ Time yourself and get a feel for how much content you need to remove or add.

☐ Jot down new ideas as they come to mind while you are reading aloud.

5. Doctor your script

☐ Be ruthless. Cut unnecessary information.

☐ Be honest. Identify sections that drag or feel boring to talk through.

☐ Be creative. Work new ideas, anecdotes, stories, or analogies into your script (don't be afraid to try things out).

6. Repeat until happy

☐ Speak through the script again.

☐ Make additional script changes.

☐ Finalize your script.

SMOOTH

MAKE YOUR VISUALS

7. Visualize your ideas

- ☐ Print out or make a blank slide template.
- ☐ Print out your script for easy reference.
- ☐ Sketch slide ideas to match your script.

8. Make your presentation tools

- ☐ Create your slide deck.
- ☐ Create speaker notes (as slide notes, on paper, or for a teleprompter).
- ☐ Create a handout (tidy up your outline from Step 3).

9. Speak and tweak

- ☐ Find a quiet space with a projector, a pen and paper, and a timer.
- ☐ Run through the entire presentation aloud with your deck, noting timing and edits required.
- ☐ Make your tweaks and repeat until you are ready to deliver it.

POLISH

AMMMAZING
OUTLINE TEMPLATE

MEANINGFUL INTRODUCTION

Begin with an attention-grabbing opening statement. Start with *why* the topic matters to your audience. Include an analogy, story, or customer example—a "hook"—that brings the topic to life. Introduce your key points. Include an appropriate introduction for yourself unless someone else will introduce you.

_____

_____

_____

_____

_____

_____

_____

MEMORABLE BODY

KEY IDEA 1

---

    a. Supporting point 1
      i. Additional detail
    b. Supporting point 2
      ii. Additional detail
    c. Supporting point 3
      iii. Additional detail

KEY IDEA 1

---

    a. _____

      i. _____

    b. _____

      ii. _____

    c. _____

      iii. _____

KEY IDEA 2

a. Supporting point 1
   i. Additional detail
b. Supporting point 2
   ii. Additional detail
c. Supporting point 3
   iii. Additional detail

KEY IDEA 2

a. _____

   i. _____

b. _____

   ii. _____

c. _____

   iii. _____

KEY IDEA 3

a. Supporting point 1
  i. Additional detail
b. Supporting point 2
  ii. Additional detail
c. Supporting point 3
  iii. Additional detail

KEY IDEA 3

a. _____

  i. _____

b. _____

  ii. _____

c. _____

  iii. _____

MOTIVATIONAL CONCLUSION

Summarize your key points. Refer to the analogy, story, or customer example from the introduction, perhaps with additional detail in light of what you have covered. Allow time for questions. Review the next steps for your audience, including resources and who to contact.

_____

_____

_____

_____

_____

_____

_____

_____

_____

_____

_____

_____

_____

AMMMAZING SLIDE DECK STRUCTURE TEMPLATE

THIS TEMPLATE SHOWS AN IDEAL slide deck structure for an aMMMazing presentation.

Meaningful Introduction

Title Slide **Presenter Names & Titles**	**Slide(s) to accompany** **your introduction**	**Agenda** 1. Topic 1 2. Topic 2 3. Topic 3

Memorable Body

Agenda 1. Topic 1 2. Topic 2 3. Topic 3		**Slide(s) for** **Topic 1**		**Agenda** 1. Topic 1 2. Topic 2 3. Topic 3	
	Slide(s) for **Topic 2**	**Agenda** 1. Topic 1 2. Topic 2 3. Topic 3			**Slide(s) for** **Topic 3**

Motivational Conclusion Slides

Summary 1. Topic 1 2. Topic 2 3. Topic 3	**Q&A** **Slide(s) to accompany** **your conclusion**	**Thank You!** **Contact information**

AMMMAZING PRESENTATION EVALUATION CHECKLIST

USE THIS CHECKLIST TO EVALUATE your presentation. Each checked item brings you one step closer to an aMMMazing presentation.

INTRODUCTION

1. Captures the audience's attention immediately
   - ☐ The opening words are purposefully chosen and well prepared.
   - ☐ The introduction includes attention-grabbing, perhaps surprising statements.
   - ☐ It does not begin with the agenda or lengthy, unnecessary self-introductions.

2. Establishes an emotional connection
   - ☐ The introduction establishes why the topic is important to the target audience.
   - ☐ The introduction reinforces relevancy with an analogy, story, quote, example, question, statistic, or news item.
   - ☐ The introduction compels the audience to listen to the rest of the presentation.

3. Sets up the rest of the presentation for success
   - ☐ The speaker previews the three main ideas or topics to be covered (the agenda).
   - ☐ The introduction length is appropriate to the overall presentation length.
   - ☐ The audience is compelled to listen to the rest of the presentation.

MEANINGFUL

BODY

1. Uses the rule of three

☐ There's a clear and distinct structure: beginning (introduction), middle (body), and end (conclusion).

☐ The information in the body is arranged around three easy-to-remember ideas.

☐ The speaker uses repetition appropriately to reinforce the presentation's key ideas.

2. Is easy to follow

☐ Information is presented in a logical and understandable manner.

☐ Speaker includes linking statements to clearly transition between sections and ideas.

☐ Any analogies, stories, quotes, or statistics are relevant and relatable.

3. Includes just the right amount of information

☐ Slides are simple and clean, complementing and reinforcing the spoken words.

☐ Speaker does not simply read words on the screen or ad-lib, unless for dramatic effect.

☐ There is an appropriate amount of information for the time available without rushing or skipping slides.

MEMORABLE

CONCLUSION

1. Summarizes main points

☐ It's clear that the body of the presentation is over and the conclusion has begun.

☐ There's a summary of all key points discussed.

☐ Speaker "closes the loop" by revisiting the analogy, story, or quotes used in the introduction.

2. Takes questions

☐ Speaker invites questions from the audience (and has allowed appropriate time).

☐ Speaker has anticipated difficult questions and has a strategy to handle them.

☐ Speaker has a well-prepared, strong closing statement to share after questions have concluded.

3. Provides call to action

☐ There's a clear call to action for the audience.

☐ There are explicit next steps: what to do, who to contact, and where to get more information.

☐ Speaker provides a one-page handout summarizing the key ideas, instead of the entire slide deck.

MOTIVATIONAL

ACKNOWLEDGMENTS

I'VE HEARD A LOT OF analogies comparing writing and publishing a book to childbirth: "It's like giving birth." "It's a labor of love." "Your book is your baby." I presume that this analogy means that delivering a baby is an unimaginable amount of effort and pain, but as I've not actually delivered a baby myself, I don't feel exactly qualified to use this comparison. However, I was in the delivery room for the birth of both of our children where I felt completely overwhelmed with equal parts uselessness and awe witnessing my wife, Rachel, bring life into the world. She handled both deliveries with so much power and grace, and I will never, ever be able to live up to those moments.

So, when I say that Rachel is the only reason this book exists, I mean it with every fiber of my being. Not only did my amazing wife support my dream of this book, she reserved me a cabin for a writing retreat, supported my countless hours of writing alone, and also entertained our beautiful children while I was working. This labor of love is only thanks to her and, just like the birth of our actual children, she has worked *way* harder than me to bring this book to life. Thank you, Rachel. I love you.

I must thank my boys, Finlay and Oran, for allowing me time to think, sketch, and write while challenging, inspiring, and entertaining me every day.

A huge thank you to the Hyland executive team who has built the most meaningful, memorable, and motivational corporate culture, ever. To illustrate, I found the time to write this book during my paid sabbatical, following strict instructions to turn off all work devices and take time to do something meaningful for myself! I would like to especially thank Bill Priemer, Ed McQuiston, and John Phelan for opportunities to collaborate on and deliver keynotes and mainstage presentations over the last fifteen years. I've been humbled and honored by their support—and that of current and former members of the Hyland executive team—in bringing this book to the world.

Thank you to David Powers, editor extraordinaire, who provided exceptional guidance early on, and to Benjamin Bykowski, who has been indispensable with his advice about presenting this work to the world through my digital presence.

Thank you to my friend Richie Muir for reading the early drafts of my manuscript and providing his songwriting insights. Thank you as well to my brother Ross Gibson for being an "always on" sounding board for ideas and encouragement. A huge thanks also to Stuart Richardson, author of the TRIM course, for his invaluable advice and guidance as I began this exciting endeavor.

Due to my analogy between presentation writing and songwriting, and my lifelong love of the band Runrig, it was a dream of mine to get this book in front of my Scottish songwriting hero, Rory Macdonald, so a huge thank you to Karin Ingram for making this happen.

And a massive thank you to all those, too numerous to mention here, who read my manuscript and provided support and encouragement along the way.

Finally, I would like to thank my team at Greenleaf Book Group for providing an exceptional amount of advice, guidance, and project management to help me share my baby with the world.

ABOUT THE AUTHOR

GLENN WAS BORN AND RAISED in South Queensferry, Scotland, where he frequented the very pub (the Hawes Inn) that legendary Scottish author Robert Louis Stevenson reportedly penned the literary classics *Kidnapped* and *Treasure Island* centuries before Glenn had his first pint there. Spending many an evening in this establishment with his friends and family inspired his dream of becoming an author, and this book is the realization of his lifelong ambition.

Glenn now lives in Avon, Ohio, with his wife, Rachel, boys, Finlay and Oran, and their West Highland Terrier, Fergus. Glenn has combined his love of speaking and technology throughout his 20-year career in various roles, achieving technology certifications from Microsoft, Citrix, and VMware, and delivering technical support, teaching OnBase software installations, and running product marketing and technology evangelism teams.

Besides public speaking and the music mentioned in this book, Glenn's passions include all things Scottish. Glenn is a proud kilt wearer, whisky sampler, bagpipe appreciator, meat pie eater, Scottish football masochist, and loves a chippy with the famous

Edinburgh salt 'n' sauce. Glenn is also a keen student of the Bible and enjoys volunteering his time to help others find purpose in life.

Like a salmon swimming back upstream, Glenn returns to Scotland whenever he has the chance to visit friends and family, explore the Highlands, and do a little fishing with his dad. One day, he plans to walk the West Highland Way with his boys, but that's a dream for another day.